JOCHEN KLEPPER (1903-1942)

CHRISTIAN POET AND WITNESS
IN TROUBLED TIMES

Jochen Klepper (1903-1942) in 1937

Photograph: akg-images

Jochen Klepper
(1903-1942)

Christian Poet and Witness in Troubled Times

J. W. Rogerson

BEAUCHIEF
ABBEY·PRESS

Published by Beauchief Abbey Press, February 2018
www.beauchiefabbeypress.org.uk

Copyright © J. W. Rogerson, 2018
The author asserts his moral right under the Copyright, Designs and Patents Act 1988, to be identified as the author of this work.

ISBN 978-0-9935499-7-7

Scripture quotations from the Authorized (King James) Version of the Bible. Rights in the Authorized Version in the United Kingdom are vested in the Crown. Reproduced by permission of the Crown's patentee, Cambridge University Press.
Scripture quotations from the Revised Standard Version of the Bible, Copyright © 1946, 1952 and 1971, by the Division of Christian Education of the National Council of the Churches of Christ in the USA, reproduced by permission, all rights reserved.

All rights reserved. No part of this publication may be reproduced, copied, stored in a retrieval system, or transmitted, in any form or by any means, without the prior written consent of the copyright holder, nor be otherwise circulated in any form of binding or cover other than that in which it is published and without a similar condition being imposed on the subsequent purchaser.

A CIP catalogue record for this title is available from the British Library.

Cover design by Michael Lindley, Truth Studio, Studio 15, Sum Studios, 1 Hartley Street, Sheffield S2 3AQ. www.truthstudio.co.uk

Printed by www.lulu.com

Introduction

I discovered Jochen Klepper quite by accident twelve or more years ago. I was using (as I still use) the German daily readings (*Die Losungen*) issued by the Moravian Community in Herrnhut and Bad Boll. These consist of two main biblical verses, one from the Old Testament and the other from the New Testament, chosen in a way that will be described later. There then follows a short prayer, or verse from a hymn or poem. Finally, two biblical passages are indicated, of which the second is part of a continuous reading from a biblical book. At the time of writing, these passages are being taken from the Acts of the Apostles, enabling users, if they so wish, to work systematically through Acts day by day. My discovery of Klepper came through the occurrence of a verse from a hymn on a day that I can no longer date. I was so struck by its beautiful simplicity and profundity that I turned to the back of the *Losungen* booklet to see where it had come from. I found the entry 'Jochen Klepper, *Kyrie*, 1938'.

The date, 1938, caught my immediate attention. By this time the true nature of the National Socialist regime in Germany was beginning to become apparent, with the imprisonment of Socialists and Communists, the persecution of Jews, and attempts to control the churches which had resulted, on the

Protestant side, in the formation of the Confessing Church. How was a Christian hymn-writer in Germany in 1938 able to write such profound words? At this stage, I did not know that Klepper had a Jewish wife, as a result of which he had been forbidden to write and publish. I did not know that together with his wife and Jewish stepdaughter, Renate, he had taken his own life in December 1942.

As I began to read books about his life and work, I discovered links with other things that interested me. For example, Klepper had studied theology at the University of Breslau (today Wrocław in Poland) where one of his teachers had been Ernst Lohmeyer. I had long been interested in Lohmeyer, and would publish a book about him in 2016. Another factor that intrigued me was that Klepper used the daily *Losungen* through which I had accidentally discovered him. Indeed, as I shall discuss later, the *Losungen* played a very important part in his life.

Klepper is, as far as I know, almost totally unknown in English-speaking circles. One reason may be that his amazingly simple poetry is almost impossible to translate into English. It seems to me that there is a need for a book about him in English, which is what is attempted in the following pages.

Thanks to the Internet I have been able to purchase and read almost everything that Klepper wrote. I have also drawn on the German biographies about him, the collections of his letters, and other studies of his work. Much in the present book will not be original in the sense of being based upon material not previously known or published. There is one sense, however, in which I hope to make a contribution, not to Klepper research, but to theology in general. Klepper had a profound sense that his life was guided by God, who spoke through the *Losungen* in good times and bad times. As a biblical scholar I want to investigate this side of his life, in order to see if it has anything to say to Christians in today's troubled world.

J. W. Rogerson
Sheffield, January 2018

CONTENTS

Frontispiece

Introduction   v

CHAPTER 1
    A Short Life   11

CHAPTER 2
    The Christian Novelist   43

CHAPTER 3
    Poet and Hymn Writer   84

CHAPTER 4
    Living in God's World as in Scripture   93

CHAPTER 5
    'Living in God's World as in Scripture'
    A Critical Appreciation   107

Bibliography   119

Biblical References   122

Index   123

Illustrations

Frontispiece
Jochen Klepper in 1937
akg-images

Jochen Klepper with his wife Hanni and his
stepdaughters, Renate and Brigitte Stein   64
*Evangelische Kirchengemeinde Gönningen; Klepper's Life
in Pictures: www.ekggoenningen.de/klepper*

A single cross marks the graves of Jochen
Klepper, his wife Hanni, and stepdaughter
Brigitte Stein in the Protestant churchyard,
Berlin-Nikolassee   64
Creative Commons, Jochen Teufel, July 2006

Katharina von Bora (1499-1552), wife of
Martin Luther   65
Oil on wood, 1529
Workshop of Lucas Cranach the Elder (1472-1553)
Uffizi Gallery, Florence

Frederick William I of Prussia (1688-1740),
King of Prussia and Elector of Brandenburg,
1712-1740   65
Oil on canvas, 1713
Samuel Theodor Gericke (1665-1729), court painter

CHAPTER 1

A Short Life

When Jochen Klepper, accompanied by his wife Hanni and daughter Reni, took his own life in December 1942, he was aged only 39. Although in his diaries he often lamented how little he felt he had achieved, he left behind two novels and the beginning of the third, as well as small volumes of hymns and poems.[1] He also left behind two diaries. Klepper was a compulsive diary writer. His main diary, published after his death under the title *Under the shadow of thy wings* and dealing with the years 1932-42, runs to over a thousand pages in the published version.[2] In addition, during a few months of compulsory military service in 1940 to 1941 he kept another diary, published under the title *Overcoming*.[3] Of his novels, the major one on the life of Frederick William I of Prussia, and

---

[1] J. Klepper, *Der Kahn der fröhlichen Leute*, (1933), cited from the edition Frankfurt: Fischer, 1955; *Der Vater. Roman eines Königs* (1937), cited from Munich: Deutsche Taschenbuch Verlag, 2003; *Die Flucht der Katharina von Bora*, Berlin: Evangelische Verlagsanstalt, 1956; *Ziel der Zeit. Die gesammelten Gedichte*, Bielefeld: Luther Verlag, 1980.
[2] J. Klepper, *Unter dem Schatten deiner Flügel. Aus den Tagebüchern der Jahre 1932-1942. Mit einem Geleitwort von Reinhold Schneider*, Stuttgart: Deutsche Verlags-Anstalt, 1955, cited hereafter as *Diary*.
[3] J. Klepper, *Überwindung. Tagebücher und Aufzeichnungen aus dem Kriege*, Stuttgart: Deutsche Verlags-Anstalt, 1958.

entitled *Der Vater* (*The Father*), runs to some 950 pages in its format by the Deutscher Taschenbuch Verlag. Klepper was a compulsive worker and was easily frustrated by the many obstacles placed in his life under Hitler's 'Third Reich'.

He was born on 22 March 1903 as Joachim Klepper, son of a Protestant pastor, Georg Klepper, in the small town of Beuthen an der Oder, today Bytom Odrzański in Poland.[4] He had two elder sisters and would later have two younger brothers. The father's Christian faith embraced the piety of the Herrnhuter Moravians, and this was conveyed to his eldest son in two ways: the use of the Herrnhuter *Losungen* and the intro-spective spiritual self-examination which would feature so prominently in the diaries. The landscape of the River Oder made a deep impression on him, as did the world of nature in general. His first published novel was about a freighter that took materials down the River Oder to the great port of Stettin (today Szczecin). His diaries and novels are full of vivid descriptions of the changing seasons, and their flora and fauna.

In October 1917, Klepper entered the Protestant Grammar School in Glogau, today Głogów, a town to the east of his birthplace and around 13 miles distant by rail. Although it was well within commuting distance of home, Klepper seems to have spent at least some of his time lodging with his French teacher, Erich Fromm, who became an important factor in his life at this stage. He also became friendly with the young wife of a local doctor, Brigitte Hacker. These relationships com-pensated for what his family home had not been able to provide. His parents were not, apparently, happily married. His mother had grown up as a Catholic and had converted to

---

[4] Beuthen was ecclesiastically part of the Old Prussian Union, and therefore neither Lutheran nor Reformed, but simply Protestant (Evangelisch).

Protestantism in order to get married. Klepper felt closer to his mother than to his father, and it has been said that the fastidious concern that he developed for his personal appearance, as well as for elegance in his domestic surroundings, derived from the influence of his mother.

Klepper remained at the grammar school until March 1922, experiencing the trauma of the German defeat in the First World War and its aftermath. Glogau was a small garrison town and an initial discharge point for returning defeated soldiers. Further, the redrawing of the boundaries of Germany and Poland after the war meant the loss to Germany of parts of Upper and Lower Silesia. The border with Poland was suddenly close to where Klepper lived. There was much social and political turmoil, and Klepper collected newspaper cuttings from this period with a view to using them as a source for a novel to be entitled *Hopelessness*.

In 1922, Klepper gained the necessary qualifications to enable him to enter university, and enrolled as a student of theology at the University of Erlangen. Here, he completed two semesters before transferring in 1923 to the University of Breslau. His ambition at this time was to become a Protestant minister. He resided in the Protestant Stift, the Johanneum, a Christian hall of residence which provided student accommodation within a strict routine of prayer and worship. A frequently visiting preacher to the Johanneum was the Professor of Systematic Theology, Rudolf Hermann, whose sermons made such a deep impression on Klepper that he was to write in his diary many years later that sermons were no longer of use to him having heard Professor Hermann preach in the Johanneum. Klepper was also profoundly influenced by Hermann's lectures on Luther and especially took to heart

Luther's teaching that Christians are at one and the same time sinners and redeemed.

Klepper also attended the lectures of Ernst Lohmeyer on the Synoptic Gospels and was a frequent visitor to the Lohmeyer household, where Melie Lohmeyer provided him with a degree of motherly reassurance. To what extent Lohmeyer's deep interest in poetry affected Klepper at this stage is hard to say. Klepper certainly showed some of his early poems to Melie Lohmeyer, who had studied in Heidelberg under Friedrich Gundolf, one of the poet Stefan George's closest disciples, but she was not impressed by them. An essay by Lohmeyer's son-in-law Wolfgang Otto, entitled 'Ernst Lohmeyer und Jochen Klepper', points to some circumstantial similarities between Lohmeyer and Klepper, without providing any hard evidence of actual influence.[5]

Klepper did not, in fact, complete his theological examinations and did not, therefore, proceed to become a minister. Several factors seem to have played a part. The rampant inflation of the 1920s put a severe strain on the finances of his father and his own resources. Secondly, apparently never robust in health (he was excused from physical education at the grammar school), he became seriously ill in 1926 and left the university at the end of that year. Also, his ambitions had begun to move in the direction of becoming a Christian poet, writer and journalist. Another factor, which was to affect his later work on Frederick William I and Katharina von Bora, was that he was overwhelmed by the great mass of material that his painstaking researches had accumulated. A dissertation on the Pietist August Hermann Francke, on the

---

[5] W. Otto, 'Ernst Lohmeyer und Jochen Klepper' in W. Otto (ed.), *Freiheit in der Gebundenheit. Zur Erinnerung an den Theologen Ernst Lohmeyer anläßlich seines 100. Geburtstages*, Göttingen: Vandenhoeck & Ruprecht, 1990, pp. 135-180.

basis of which Klepper hoped to gain his Licentiate in Theology, was never completed for this reason. [6]

In a letter to his Breslau professor, Hermann, dated 24 April 1928, Klepper wrote that his study of theology had been an essential preparation for his work as a Christian writer and poet, and in June 1929 he was able to inform Hermann that his relatively good financial position at that moment had enabled him to repay the grants he had received to enable him to live and study at the Johanneum.[7]

An offer of a job in Breslau, working for the Protestant Press Agency for Silesia, opened up a new chapter in his life. It meant a break with his family in Beuthen and especially with his father, who had hoped that he would enter the church's ministry.

The main function of the Protestant Press Agency was to publish a weekly magazine for church congregations, entitled 'Our Church'. Its circulation was 43,000 copies. In addition, the Agency supplied news items to the general press of the area on church matters. Klepper contributed regular articles. In addition, he began to work for the newly developing medium of radio broadcasting, which had begun in 1924 with the Silesian Broadcasting Company, whose theoretical audience was over four million. His first broadcast, on 12 June 1927, marked the 200th anniversary of the death of the Pietist, August Hermann Francke. Klepper had already done some work on Francke during his theological studies and,

---

[6] See the observation by E. G. Riemschneider in E. G. Riemschneider (ed.), *Jochen Klepper. Briefwechsel 1925-1942*, Stuttgart: Deutsche Verlags-Anstalt, 1973, p. 126, who comments on Klepper's 'unerschöpfliches Materialsammeln und die nicht enden wollen Vorstudien' and adds 'Schon als Student hatte Klepper, besonders bei seiner Lizentiatenarbeit, mit dieser Schwierigkeit zu kämpfen'.
[7] Riemschneider, *Briefwechsel*, pp. 30-31.

interestingly, would write again about Francke in his masterpiece on Frederick William I of Prussia. Another avenue for publication of his writings was the Social Democratic journal 'Forwards', for which he wrote in 1928. This association with the Social Democratic Party would soon land him in trouble with the growing influence exerted by the National Socialist movement.

On 26 April 1929 Klepper met a Jewish widow 13 years his senior, named Johanna Stein, although it is unlikely that this was the very first time that they had encountered each other.[8] This meeting would profoundly affect Klepper's life, and lead to his self-chosen death. Johanna Stein was the widow of a Jewish lawyer who had died in 1925 at the age of 38, leaving her with two daughters, Brigitte born in 1920 and Renate born two years later. She had a large house in Breslau and was glad to accept Klepper as a lodger. The Steins were an assimilated, largely non-practising Jewish family, although this would not later protect them from the perverse anti-Semitic zeal of the National Socialists.

Johanna, or 'Hanni' Klepper called her, was an educated, cultured and well-read woman, and to this extent she shared many interests with her younger lodger. At the age of 39 she also probably supplied a female reassurance such as had earlier been supplied by women such as Melie Lohmeyer. However, she supplied much more than emotional support. Around the beginning of 1927 Klepper's father, Georg, had a stroke, and Klepper rallied to help his mother and the family

---

[8] In a letter to Hermann dated 31 March 1931, Klepper said that he had met Hanni in Paris and Berlin when both, for different reasons, were visiting fashion houses. Klepper was researching for his novel *The Great Female Director*, and Hanni was related to the fashion house Gerstel. See Riemschneider, *Briefwechsel*, p. 34. Klepper adds that Hanni had spoken about fashion on the radio.

support him and pay for the care that he needed. The growing inflation and the worldwide financial collapse of 1929 drastically reduced the father's income. Klepper himself was now earning very little and found himself in great financial difficulty as he tried to support the family in Beuthen. The trust between him and Hanni grew to the point where Hanni, who came from a wealthy family and had assets at her disposal, began to make increasingly large loans to Klepper. With trust came genuine love, and they were married at a civil ceremony on 28 March 1931. Ironically in the circumstances, marriage to a Jewish woman was the last straw for Klepper's father and family, with whom Klepper would now have little contact until shortly before the death of Georg Klepper at the end of October 1934.

The importance of Klepper's marriage to Johanna Stein cannot be underestimated. While it had its drawbacks (Hanni was unable to bear any more children, and Klepper longed to have at least a son, and they were both to suffer from the anti-Semitism of the Hitler era), Klepper never regretted the step that he had taken. Time and again in his diaries he declared how much his marriage meant to him, and when it was later suggested that he should divorce Hanni and free himself from the burden of being married to a non-Aryan, he rejected the idea out of hand. For her part, Hanni played an important role in Klepper's life and work. She maintained the kind of orderly and elegant family home that Klepper desired. She gave him archival support as he researched the material for his great novel on Frederick William I, and would stay up until the small hours of the morning typing Klepper's submissions to a film company that toyed with the idea of filming part of his novel, before declining to do so. Klepper seems to have made no overt attempt to convert his wife to Christianity. The family celebrated Christmas, as did many assimilated Jewish families, and Hanni sometimes accompanied her husband to church services. It was, therefore, a great joy when Hanni decided to be baptised. This took place on 18 December 1938 in Mariendorf, and was followed immediately by the church blessing of the marriage.

During the years before his civil marriage in 1931, Klepper was working on a novel entitled, *The Great Female Director*. This was in addition to his regular work as a broadcaster and journalist. The novel was never published, but a summary is given by Rita Thalmann.[9] It is not an easy plot to follow, and it is noteworthy for its apparent concentration upon Jewish matters. Its two main characters are the daughter of the Mayor of Glogau, named Leonie, and her friend Valeska, a baptised Protestant theologian of Jewish parentage. Both characters are bullied by their female classmates at school, Valeska on account of her ugliness. Leonie retreats into the inner world of designing clothes for puppets, which lays the foundation for her later career as a successful fashion designer. Her success depends on a Jewish fashion house, to the displeasure of her parents. With the war and its aftermath and the demise of the Jewish fashion house that marketed her designs, Leonie launches a new career in films, eventually finding fulfilment in marriage to a wool merchant.

Valeska follows an academic career path, specializing in Spinoza and the history of piety. She is interned in Switzerland during the war and then works as a translator, trying to present the main characters of the Bible as they might be in modern circumstances. After the failure of this enterprise she works as a receptionist for a dentist and as a librarian before finding herself living in poverty in the Jewish ghetto in

---

[9] R. Thalmann, *Jochen Klepper. Ein Leben zwischen Idyllen und Katastrophen*, Munich: Kaiser Verlag, 1977, pp. 59-61.

Prague. Here she is met by her friend Leonie to whom she recounts her despair at her life and the state of the world. Leonie takes her to Ferney-Voltaire in the Jura Mountains near Geneva, where she presumably dies.

As summarised, the plot seems quite bleak and there is no way of knowing how Klepper who, on the evidence of his later writings was a master of vivid descriptive narrative, brought it to life. It seems that Leonie and Valeska were meant by Klepper to stand for two types of person, what he called 'the chosen' (Valeska) and 'the blinded' (Leonie), the difference being that Leonie is unable to see reality beyond the material things of the world and is confined to its conventions. Valeska appears to embody Klepper's belief in a life dedicated to and guided by God that breaks out of human conventions, however much outward circumstances might seem to deny this.[10] One can only guess at the inner conflicts of Klepper's life at this time that the novel sought to express, and in some ways it was prophetic of his own life. Initial attempts to find a publisher were not successful.

In October 1931 Klepper moved to Berlin to look for work and a house, leaving Hanni and her daughters in Breslau. The National Socialists had made gains in Silesia, and Klepper had come under increasing criticism on account of his Protestant faith and his membership of the Social Democratic Party. His daughters had begun to be victimised as anti-Semitism took on a more public face. In Berlin his desperate search for employment brought many disappointments. For example, he spent a lot of time rewriting *The Great Female Director* under a new title seven times, only to have it rejected.[11] A ray of hope

---

[10] A third character is mentioned, a baptised Catholic hairdresser of Jewish parentage, who finds fame in Paris. He represents the cult of personal beauty and is described as 'the rejected', *der Verworfene*.
[11] Klepper to Hermann, 13 August 1933, in Riemschneider, *Briefweschel*, p. 38.

eventually pierced the darkness. The Deutsche Verlags-Anstalt agreed to accept a new novel from Klepper with an advance of 5,000 marks, a monthly allowance of 300 marks, and a royalty of 15 per cent on sales. This novel was *Der Kahn der fröhlichen Leute (The Barge of the Joyful People)*, which Klepper wrote in the space of a few months towards the end of 1932, finishing it on 2 November, Hanni's birthday.[12] Although it will be considered in a later chapter, it can be said here that it is a charming story about a freighter on the River Oder, which is inherited by an orphan named Wilhelmine, who counters the rampant unemployment and economic depression of the 1920s by imaginatively giving space on the freighter to a group of actors and a pony, bringing hope and entertainment to the people and the places where the freighter berths. In writing it Klepper drew on his intimate knowledge of the landscape and customs of the Oder region, where he had grown up, and the newspaper cuttings that he had collected about the economic and political situation there in the 1920s.

Two days after finishing his book, *Der Kahn*, Klepper was offered a job by Harald Braun, broadcasting on Berlin Radio (Berliner Funk). Braun, whom Klepper had first met while working for the Protestant Press Agency, was to be a great help to Klepper in the difficult years ahead. The son of a Protestant minister, Braun later became a distinguished film writer and producer. With the promised income from *Der Kahn* and employment in broadcasting and journalism, Klepper's immediate financial problems were considerably eased. Six months earlier, in March 1932, Klepper had been joined in Berlin by Hanni, and later by the daughters, the family taking up residence in the Südende suburb of Berlin.

---

[12] *Diary*, p. 30. J. Klepper, *Der Kahn der fröhlichen Leute*, [1933], Frankfurt: Fischer Bücherei, 1955.

Klepper's work at Berlin Radio lasted for only 30 weeks. Even Harald Braun could not save Klepper from dismissal, following the seizure of power by the National Socialists and Hitler at the beginning of 1933. He was informed of his dismissal as he arrived for work on 7 June 1933. Braun, however, continued to do what he could for Klepper. Possibilities included continuing his reviewing, but anonymously, at 60% of his previous fees, and work at the Ullstein publishers. Thus was established a pattern that characterised the next five years, with Klepper's family living on the occasional income from anonymous reviews and articles, and the royalties from *Der Kahn*. It was during these years that the work on Klepper's masterpiece, *Der Vater* was begun and completed.

The idea for writing this book came to him on 13 September 1933, but it had been prepared, among other things, by his visits to Potsdam, the capital city built by Frederick William I, and a viewing of the portraits painted by the king and displayed in the Berlin Stadtschloss. The research undertaken for writing the novel was all-encompassing, including the use of written material, such as the published memoirs of Frederick William's eldest daughter Wilhelmine, visits to the various castles and stately homes associated with Frederick William and the family, and a study of the standard histories of that period. One of Klepper's sources was the book on the Hohenzollern family, which was published in 1933 by Reinhold Schneider.[13] At one stage, Klepper was fearful that Schneider had beaten him to it, and that his own book would be redundant. He need not have worried. Schneider devoted only 100 pages to Frederick William I, concentrating on Frederick William's political and economic achievements, and

---

[13] R. Schneider, *Die Hohenzollern. Tragik und Königtum*, Leipzig: Verlag Jakob Hegner, 1933.

leaving entirely untouched the intimate family and personal details that are found in Klepper's book. However, the appearance of Schneider's work led to contact between the two authors, who were roughly the same age, and to a friendship that endured until Klepper took his life.[14]

Der Vater will be considered in detail in a later chapter, but it is necessary to note here Klepper's motives and intentions in writing the book, for he was living at a time when a dominant leader, Adolf Hitler, was claiming to be able to rebuild a Germany whose empire would last for a thousand years. It was evident, even in 1933, that this process would be based upon a brutality and intolerance and a glorification of power that were a denial of Christian values. Klepper asked the question, 'How can a Christian be the father of his country? How can he carry the responsibility of ruling and reconstruction in the consciousness of being a sinner?'[15] The aim of the novel would be to answer that question in the portrayal of Frederick William I. The novel had from the outset the intention to subvert and oppose the aims and procedures of the Hitler regime. It is an irony that the novel proved to be a bestseller, even in National Socialist circles.

The routine of Klepper's life was disturbed in the first half of 1934 by the possibility that parts of the novel *Der Vater* might be made into a film by Universum Film (UFA). This required Klepper to break off from researching and writing the novel, so that he could produce screenplay versions of the first part of the book. Those responsible at UFA seem to have made unreasonable demands on Klepper to produce material to meet unrealistic deadlines, to which he responded, helped by

---

[14] Their correspondence can be found in Riemschneider, B*riefwechsel*, pp.61-157.
[15] 'Wie kann ein Christ ein Landesvater sein? Herrschen, Verantwortung tragen, Aufbauen in Sündenbewusstsein?' *Diary*, p. 116.

secretarial assistance from Hanni. All this was to no avail. On 7 March 1934, Klepper was informed that the film would require much expensive period costume and staging, and that the timetable of the studios was such that no slot would be available in the near future for the filming to be concluded. The letter rather cynically concluded 'you can thus use your immediate time as you wish'.[16]

Unfortunately, this was not the end of this unhappy episode with UFA. A second edition of *Der Kahn* had been printed and now there was talk of this book being filmed. Once again, Klepper was faced with producing material to unrealistic deadlines. On 22 March 1934, Klepper was at his writing desk until 3.00 am, while Hanni typed until 1.00 am.[17] Once again, Klepper again found himself caught between promises that were never kept, but which demanded from him much lost time in telephone calls, meetings and the production of draft film scripts. Finally, on 6 April 1934, he gave up on the possibility of any filming, and withdrew from the negotiations. The negotiations had robbed him of time and vitality. He had written little more of *Der Vater*. On 10 April, the first day for some time that he had heard nothing about films, he was able to write ten pages. The first section was completed on 13 April. A letter was received from UFA on 17 April, a letter described by Klepper as 'arrogant and deceitful', confirming the end of the negotiations.[18] From then on, Klepper was able to concentrate on the novel, combining this work with the occasional anonymous reviews and articles that made funds possible for him. Whether or not the inconsiderate treatment that Klepper endured at the hands of UFA was typical of the film industry in general (it is not unknown for

---

[16] 'Sie können also über Ihre nächste Zeit verfügen, wie Sie wollen', *Diary*, p. 158.
[17] *Diary*, p. 161.
[18] *Diary*, p. 172.

publishers to treat academic authors in not dissimilar ways), Klepper put his experience down to the attitude of people who lived in Berlin. 'Now I have learned for the first time what "Berlin" is, and see with horror how one can waste one's life and gifts when one does not keep one's ambition and desire for success under some sort of control'.[19]

Towards the end of 1934, the Kleppers decided to sell the house belonging to Hanni in Breslau, and to use the money to build a new house for the family in Berlin. This would save them from paying rent, and also have tax advantages. They would also be able to let part of the house and have some income in that way. A site was purchased in the Südende part of Berlin, which was inexpensive because it had been neglected and was overgrown with trees and shrubs. Klepper hoped that as many trees as possible could be saved.[20] On 8 June 1935, Klepper could note in the diary that the walls were completed and that a good impression could be gained of what the house would look like: 'It looks like a house in the forest.'[21] By early September the house was almost finished.[22]

In the summer of 1936, the Olympic Games were held in Berlin, and the National Socialist regime was host to many nations of the world. Anti-Semitism was masked as much as possible and the regime presented Germany as a prosperous, forward-looking nation. Klepper composed seven Olympic Sonnets. They were not published at the time and would have got him into serious trouble if they had been published.[23]

---

[19] 'Jetzt lerne ich erst kennen, was "Berlin" ist, und sehe mit Schrecken, wie man sein Leben und Begabung vertun kann, wenn man seinen Ehrgeist und seinen Geschäftsgeist nicht im Zaume hält', *Diary*, p. 168.
[20] *Diary*, p. 245-6.
[21] *Diary*, p. 262. 'Es liegt wie ein Haus im Walde'.
[22] *Diary*, p. 281.
[23] See J. Klepper, *Ziel der Zeit*, Bielefeld: Luther-Verlag, 1980, pp. 31-8, for text.

Klepper was deeply distressed by the way in which the main sites in Berlin had been bedecked with flags and illuminations, all of which represented an enormous lie, masking an awful reality. The *Losung* for 2 August 1936, when Klepper began to compose the sonnets, was from Jeremiah 23.28:

> The prophet that hath a dream,
> let him tell a dream;
> and he that hath my word,
> let him speak my word faithfully.

One imagines that Klepper saw the outward show of the Berlin Olympic decorations as a dream, which needed to be confronted by the truth.[24]

Each of the seven Olympic Sonnets is named after a site in Berlin: the Brandenburg Gate, the Pariser Platz just inside the Brandenburg Gate, St Hedwig's Church, the Opera, the Olympic flame in front of the Royal Palace,[25] the Museum, the Bridge over the River Spree, towards the top of Unter den Linden, and the Zeughaus (arsenal). The poems hark back to the wars that had brought victors to these places, victors at the expense of the victims of war. The banners and flags suggest a peaceful future for the world, yet conceal an ideology that can only lead to war. For Klepper, it is only the coming of night, when the decorations can no longer be seen and the illuminations are switched off, that beauty returns to Berlin.[26]

Almost a year earlier, on 30 August 1935, Klepper had written the first of his four 'King's Poems'.[27] Each poem was preceded

---

[24] *Diary*, p. 367.
[25] i.e., the Berliner Schloss at the top of Unter den Linden which was badly destroyed in the war and later demolished.
[26] *Diary*, p. 367, 'Die Nacht verdeckte alles Häßliche. Die Linden, Berlin war so schön wie noch nie'.
[27] *Ziel der Zeit*, pp. 39-42.

by a biblical verse, the first being from Isaiah 33.17-18, beginning, 'Thine eyes shall see the king in his beauty.' These poems contrasted the futility of a regime that looked to last for a thousand years and that sought to convert sickles into swords, with a kingly rule exercised in the awareness of sinfulness and of the judgement to which rulers would be subjected. Kings who do not find Christ's Golgotha do not find their own thrones.[28]

Work on *Der Vater* continued throughout 1935 and 1936, and the book grew to enormous proportions, probably because of Klepper's inability to cope with the mass of material he had accumulated. He wanted to publish the book in two volumes. The publisher refused, and the book had to be shortened considerably.[29] It was finally published in February 1937, and a month later Klepper was informed that he had been suspended from membership of the State Literary Chamber (*Reichsschrifttumskammer*), membership of which was necessary if a person wished to write and publish.

Klepper's suspension and exclusion had the effect that some booksellers and reviewers were reluctant to handle the book.[30] However, this did not prevent its success. During Klepper's lifetime, 85,000 copies were sold[31] and even the aged ex-Kaiser Wilhelm II in exile in the Netherlands distributed 30 copies as Christmas presents in 1937![32] That the author of such a successful work should be banned from writing was an absurdity that even the National Socialist regime appreciated,

---

[28] 'Wenn Könige dein Golgotha nicht fanden, so fanden sie auch ihre Throne nicht' *Ziel der Zeit*, p. 40, last two lines of poem II.
[29] See *Briefwechsel*, p. 75, where the editor remarks that the book was having to be shortened by 100 pages yet again.
[30] Klepper to Rudolf Hermann on 17 July 1937 in *Briefswechsel*, p. 43.
[31] Klepper to Walter Tappolet, 23 February 1942 in *Briefswechsel*, p. 192.
[32] Klepper to Reinhold Schneider on 15 January 1938 in *Briefweschsel*, p. 97.

and it led to a suspension of the execution of the order for Klepper's exclusion. Klepper was informed of this in June 1937 and noted in his diary that representations on his behalf had even sought the assistance of Hermann Göring.[33] The outcome was that Klepper was not prevented from writing and publishing, although he was obliged to submit his material to the authorities for their approval. The immediate result of this was the publication in 1938 of two small books that were the result of his researches on the life of Frederick William. In May 1938, there appeared *In Tormentis Pinxit*, in which were reproduced twenty-five paintings that Frederick William had painted in the years shortly before his death in 1740, together with fourteen letters to members of his family and other royal and important persons. Painting had become a kind of therapy for Frederick William at the end of his life and revealed a unique feature of his personality.[34]

The other book, which appeared in August 1938, was entitled *The King and the Quiet in the Land*.[35] The phrase 'the quiet in the land' (*die Stillen im Lande*) went back to Luther's translation of Psalm 35.20:

> Denn sie trachten schaden zuthun,
> Und suchen falsche Sachen wider die Stillen im Lande
>
> (They strive to inflict harm, and seek false things against
> the quiet in the land).

The phrase 'the quiet in the land' came to denote the Pietists of the late and seventeenth and eighteenth centuries, including the Moravians led by Count Nikolaus von Zinzendorf. The

---

[33] *Diary*, pp. 463-4.
[34] J. Klepper, *In Tormentis Pinxit. Briefe und Bilder des Soldatenkönigs*, Stuttgart: Deutsche Verlags-Anstalt, 1938.
[35] J. Klepper, *Der König und die Stillen im Lande*, Witten/Berlin: Eckart-Verlag, 1938.

subtitle of the book was 'Encounters of Frederick William I with August Hermann Francke, Gotthilf August Francke, Johann Anastasius Freylinghausen and Nikolaus Ludwig Graf von Zinzendorf'. The book included not only letters to and from the king, but also accounts of conversations, for example, arising from the king's visit to the famous orphanage (*Waisenhaus*) in Halle in 1713.

A month later, in September 1938, a collection of Klepper's hymns was published under the title *Kyrie*.[36] The invitation to contribute some poems for a small anthology of church poetry had come from the Eckart publishing house in January 1935,[37] and Klepper was glad to receive it. He began to compose the sublime verses, which will be considered in a later chapter, from time to time, as opportunity allowed.

Klepper and his family received disturbing news early in 1938. Hitler and his architect Albert Speer had devised plans for a massive reshaping of Berlin, in order to make it fit to be the capital of the New Germany Hitler intended to fashion. The Klepper house stood in the way of the development, and was planned to become part of a new railway complex in the Südende suburb of Berlin. The house was to be purchased compulsorily under a law effective from 1 February 1938.[38] The Kleppers had lived in their new house for less than three years. Now they had to begin all over again, with disruption to their finances and to Klepper's writing. A new site was found in Nikolassee, near the parish church. In January 1939 Klepper complained to Reinhold Schneider about the time-consuming negotiations with banks, officials, solicitors and the

---

[36] J. Klepper, *Kyrie. Geistliche Lieder* [1938], Bielefeld: Luther-Verlag, 1950.
[37] *Diary*, p. 231.
[38] *Briefwechsel*, p. 101.

police.[39] It was not until May 1939 that the family was able to move into the new house.

The idea of a house of his own was very important for Klepper. Having grown up in a minister's manse, he had had hopes of becoming a minister and living in his own manse, before he felt led to devote his life to Christian writing. In these new circumstances he still hoped for a house of his own, and Hanni was an important factor here, not only because her financial assets helped Klepper to obtain what he could not have achieved on his own, but because her domestic management met Klepper's need for stability and sophistication. But an earthly home was only an anticipation for Klepper of an eternal home; and another complex of ideas became bound up with this anticipation.

Klepper had long had a deep regard for Martin Luther, helped by the lectures of his Breslau teacher, Rudolf Hermann. In 1935 he recommended to Reinhold Schneider a book on Luther by Rudolf Thiel, which had helped Klepper to a deeper understanding of Luther's inner struggles.[40] That he might write a book on Luther was beyond his competence. However, he began to toy with the idea of writing a book about Luther's wife, Katharina von Bora. She had enabled Luther to have a house and a household, which could be an inspiration for Klepper and others, as well as an anticipation of the eternal house beyond this world. Klepper's first thoughts about this occurred to him on 9 August 1935 when the *Losung* from Isaiah 37.31 mentioned 'the house of Judah and the remnant that remained'. It reminded him of the things that remained to be completed on his Südende house, the one that would be

---

[39] *Briefwechsel*, p. 122.
[40] Klepper to Schneider, 14 November 1935, in *Briefwechsel*, p.71. See R. Thiel, *Luther, von 1483 bis 1522*, Berlin: Paul Neff Verlag, 1933.

compulsorily purchased. He wrote in his diary that they (presumably he and Hanni) had spoken for the first time about Katharina von Bora, and that the idea of the first Protestant manse became more and more appealing.[41] Once the great work on Frederick William was completed, Klepper's energies, when not distracted by the many difficulties that lay ahead, would be directed towards a book about Katharina entitled, *Das ewige Haus (The Eternal House)*. In fact, only the first part was completed, and published after his death, under the title, *The Flight of Katharina von Bora*.[42]

Among the distractions that lay ahead was a renewed interest in filming parts of the book on Frederick William, and the film rights were obtained by Tobis, one of the four main film companies in Germany. Klepper was understandably reluctant to become as deeply involved in the project as he had been on the first, fruitless occasion, but he could not avoid some involvement. Once again, the outcome was disappointing, and in a letter to his friends Kurt and Juliane Meschke on 24 August 1938, Klepper reflected bitterly on the feeble excuses for not proceeding with the filming [43]

Klepper had met pastor Dr Kurt Meschke (1901-71) in 1929, while working for the Protestant Press Agency. In August 1930, Meschke had married Eva-Juliane Anker, and for the next twelve years the Kleppers and Meschkes corresponded regularly. Juliane, like Hanni Klepper, was Jewish, and as a result her husband was dismissed from his position as student

---

[41] 'Aber das erste Pfarrhaus zieht mich natürlich mehr und mehr an', *Diary*, p. 274.
[42] J. Klepper, *Die Flucht der Katharina von Bora, Aus dem Nachlaß herausgegeben und eingeleitet von Karl Pagel*, Berlin: Evangelische Verlagsanstalt, 1956 [Stuttgart: Deutsche Verlags-Anstalt, 1951]
[43] J. Klepper, *Gast und Fremdling. Briefe an Freunde* (ed. Eva-Juliane Meschke), Witten/Berlin: Eckart Verlag, 1960, p. 205.

chaplain in Danzig in September 1933, on account of the non-Aryan marriage. As things became more difficult for the Meschkes, they sought to emigrate to Sweden. After several disappointments they succeeded in leaving Germany on 11 February 1939. Their presence in Sweden would play an important part in Klepper's unsuccessful attempts to get his younger stepdaughter Reni out of Germany. Also, after Brigitte's successful emigration to England, they were a postal link between Brigitte and her family, especially after the outbreak of war. Shortly before the Meschkes left, they were able to visit the new, but not yet completed house at Nikolassee. The new house was ready for occupation on 22 May 1939.[44]

Brigitte was not to experience the new house. In April 1939 she obtained a visa and passport to emigrate to England, and on 9 May Klepper recorded the events of her departure.[45] Hanni went with her daughter by train to Hamburg, where she embarked for the passage to England via Le Havre, from where she sent a postcard. Klepper and Reni met Hanni at the Lehrter railway station on her return at 11.00 pm that evening. The departure of Brigitte was clearly a blow for the family, although mixed with relief at her safety. The farewells were undertaken stoically, and Brigitte kept up a regular correspondence after her arrival and settling in Croydon.

The removal of the Kleppers to Nikolassee brought Klepper into closer contact with the Church than previously. The assistant pastor in Nikolassee was Dr Karl Lilge, a member of the Confessing Church, a movement for which Klepper had previously had little sympathy, on account of what Klepper held to be its wrong involvement in political matters. On

---

[44] *Gast und Fremdling*, p. 168.
[45] *Diary*, p. 765.

Sunday 9 July 1939, Klepper referred in his diary to an amazingly good and mature sermon by the young pastor on 1 Peter 3.8-17 about the sufferings of the Christian community, then and now.[46] Klepper's feeling of being at home in the congregation at Nikolassee became an important source of strength and comfort.

With the emigration of Brigitte, the future of Reni began to weigh on Klepper's mind. On 12 May 1939, shortly after Brigitte's departure, Klepper noted in his diary that those who knew Reni could not understand why she did not want to leave also.[47] Nevertheless, attempts to arrange for Reni to emigrate increasingly claimed Klepper's attention, especially as rumours about the deportation of Jews began to be confirmed by events. Klepper initially turned for help to Walter Tappolet, a Swiss church musician, whom he had come to know because one of the Klepper hymns had made such an impression in Switzerland that there was a desire for it to be included in a new hymnal.[48] Tappolet and Klepper were able to meet on 15 July 1939 at a church music event in Spandau, and Klepper brought Renate with him, although nothing was said about emigration at the time. However, Klepper took advantage of his acquaintance with Tappolet to see whether, through him, Reni's emigration to Switzerland might be arranged. Tappolet could not have been more helpful, but the cumbersome bureaucracy and reluctance of the Swiss authorities to offend Germany meant that the attempt failed. The surviving correspondence between Klepper and Tappolet chronicles the false hopes, the delays and, finally, the disappointment of failure that both sides endured. The final

---

[46] *Diary*, p. 775.
[47] 'Ich habe doch hier alles, was ich brauche und wünsche - und mehr', *Diary*, p. 767.
[48] *Briefwechsel*, p. 163.

blow fell on 10 May 1940.[49] A month later, on 9 June 1940, Reni was baptised in an impressive service at Nikolassee. That this was not a response to the Swiss disappointment is shown by the fact that Reni had announced her decision to be baptised in April, and had added that had her mother not kept her baptism in 1938 a secret, she would gladly have been baptised at the same time.[50] Attempts to get Reni to Sweden would feature prominently later, and this failure would lead Klepper, Hanni and Reni to take their own lives in December 1942.

Near the end of 1940, Klepper was conscripted into military service and from 3 December 1940 to 8 October 1941 served in a support unit just behind the front line. He kept a diary of his time in the army which was published after his death under the title *Overcoming*.[51]

Klepper's attitude to the war and to military service will be very difficult for English readers to appreciate. One would expect Klepper, who had suffered so much from the Hitler regime, to be strongly against the war and military service; but this was not so. He had an innate conservatism that not only made him dislike the Confessing Church's open opposition to Hitler, but which also made him loyal to his country, however much he disliked its rulers and their aims. And there were other reasons. He felt a deep attachment to the country which Frederick William had done so much to found, and to Silesia, where he had grown up and which Frederick William's son, Frederick II, had won for Prussia. The castles and royal palaces which he had visited in his researches were all part of his country's heritage to which he felt bound. There was also a practical reason; Klepper believed that serving in the army

---

[49] *Briefwechsel*, p. 185.
[50] *Diary*, p. 870.
[51] J. Klepper, *Überwindung. Tagebücher und Aufzeichnungen aus dem Kriege*, Stuttgart: Deutsche Verlags-Anstalt, 1958.

would help him to protect Hanni and Reni; that this demonstration of his loyalty to his country would outweigh the fact of their non-Aryan heritage.[52] 'I was willingly a soldier', Klepper wrote to Rudolf Hermann in October 1941, after his dismissal from the army on account of his non-Aryan marriage.[53]

Klepper's military service revealed some of the paradoxes of his complex personality. Here was a man whose frustrations at being unable to get on with his writing were constantly aired in his diary; yet he happily spent ten months in the army without complaining about what that was doing to hinder his work. He was also disappointed when he was dismissed from the army because of his non-Aryan wife. Again, here was a shy man who constantly refused invitations to attend and address meetings as his fame as a writer and poet began to spread, but who greatly enjoyed the comradeship of his fellow soldiers. The army taught him how to get a good night's sleep, and his military service helped him to overcome the insomnia that often plagued his life.

Klepper's diary is in itself an important contribution to history, written as it is from the standpoint of an ordinary soldier possessed of great gifts of observation and facility in language. Although it gives details of the military operations at the front, ahead of Klepper's support unit, its greatest interest lies in the vivid descriptions of the countryside and the reception of the German army as it moved through Bulgaria and Romania and then crossed into the Ukrainian Soviet Republic. Klepper's journey east reached the town of Poltava on the eastern side of the River Dnieper before his discharge sent him back on a journey by rail through Lemberg

---

[52] *Briefwechsel*, p. 151.
[53] 'Ich war sehr gerne Soldat' in *Briefwechsel*, p. 56.

and Kraków to Berlin. There are vivid descriptions of the hospitality offered to the advancing German troops by the inhabitants of simple, undeveloped villages. The great River Dnieper impressed him particularly, given that he had grown up in the basin of the River Oder, and was intimately acquainted with its landscape and customs. Within the Soviet Union Klepper noted how churches had been turned into dance halls and how, now that the Communists were no longer in control, religious icons had appeared in homes as though they had always been there;[54] and how a German army chaplain, assisted by an Orthodox priest, had administered baptism to children who had been denied it under the Communists.[55]

Exactly what Klepper was doing during his military service is not easy to discover. His biographers say more about what was happening to Hanni and Reni in Berlin than what Klepper was actually doing in the army. The war diary is not particularly informative either, presumably because Klepper assumed that his readers would know what the support unit did. From the few references to his work in the war diary, it is possible to deduce that Klepper was attached to the staff of the adjutant of the unit, and had an administrative role. He was presumably responsible for requisitioning equipment, and munitions, and dealing with such matters as the collection and distribution of post, an important factor in the morale of the troops at the front. Klepper and several companions worked from a converted bus, which served as a mobile office. On some occasions they slept in houses and ate meals provided by the villagers where they happened to be. On other occasions they slept in tents close to the bus which was camouflaged or concealed. Klepper also seems to have been

---

[54] *Überwindung*, p. 180.
[55] *Überwindung*, p. 152.

asked to provide regular reports of the progress of the division, which were circulated among senior officers.

The fact that Klepper was the author of *Der Vater* made a big difference to his army service. A number of officers had read the book, and treated Klepper with great respect. He was asked to give talks to officers and other ranks about Frederick William, occasions which were seen as important for the morale of the troops. He was sometimes accorded special treatment by being taken by one of the majors to see parts of the front normally accessible only to combatants. When the National Socialist regime decided that soldiers with non-Aryan spouses were not fit for military service, strenuous efforts were made on Klepper's behalf by his senior officers for him to be made an exception. Another side of his ability was recognized when he was entrusted with the work of being a spiritual adviser.

The regular correspondence with Hanni that Klepper maintained informed him about the bombing in Berlin, the introduction of the yellow star to be worn by Reni, but not yet Hanni, and the fact that her Jewishness meant that Reni could not boat upon the Nikolassee. Also, there was news about how Jews were being conscripted for factory work. Klepper's military service was interrupted in April and May 1941 by the death of his mother, whose funeral he was given permission to attend. He was absent from his unit from 30 April to 21 May, including the considerable travelling time involved.[56] From the end of July Hanni's letters became more and more anxious as she described the tightening of restrictions on what Jews could do, and the increasing burdens placed upon them.

---

[56] *Überwindung*, pp. 26-31.

On his return to civilian life Klepper was filled with anxiety for the future of Reni, and was grateful for the fact that the Meschkes in Sweden had begun to seek a way of allowing Reni to join them.[57] For his part, Klepper made contact with the chaplain of the Swedish community in Berlin and advised the Meschkes about some contacts he had with the Swedish representatives of the YMCA.[58] He also wrote on 25 October 1941 to the Minister of the Interior, Dr Wilhelm Frick (1877-1946), who would later be tried and executed at the Nuremberg Military Tribunal. In his letter Klepper mentioned his books on Frederick William, the purchase of the film rights by Tobis, and his military service, and hoped that the regime would grant some protection to his wife and daughter.[59] Two days later came a reply from Frick's office signed by Dr Langsdorff. It acknowledged the receipt of Klepper's letter and assured him that he need have no anxieties about his stepdaughter. She would not be affected by the plans for the evacuation of Jews.[60] This 'protection letter' proved to be very valuable for the next year, during which the attempts to obtain a visa for Reni to go to Sweden continued.

In November 1941 Klepper was devastated by what happened to Joachim Gottschalk. Gottschalk was a leading German film star, but he had married a Jewish actress named Meta Wolff. The propaganda minister, Josef Goebbels, gave Gottschalk an ultimatum. If he wished to continue making films, he must divorce his wife. Gottschalk refused, because this would mean deportation for Meta and their son. On 6 November 1941 the family took their own lives by gas poisoning. Klepper now feared that similar action would be taken against artists and

---

[57] *Gast und Fremdling*, p. 277.
[58] *Gast und Fremdling*, p. 279.
[59] *Briefwechsel*, pp. 227-8.
[60] 'Sie fällt nicht unter die Maßnahmen, die in Verbindung mit dem Evakuierungsprogramm zur Zeit durchgeführt werden', *Briefwechsel*, p. 229.

performers.⁶¹ In discussions between Klepper, Hanni and Reni, Reni said that her friend Elisabeth who worked in the same factory, and she, had decided that suicide would be preferable to deportation.⁶² For the moment, the 'protection letter' kept Reni safe from deportation; but the Gottschalk affair put the possibility of suicide firmly on the agenda for the Kleppers. On 4 December 1941 Klepper spent two hours with a solicitor (*Justizrat*) discussing testamentary arrangements in the case of his and Hanni's suicide.⁶³ On 5 December he noted rumours that the New Year would see the introduction of compulsory divorce for those with non-Aryan spouses.⁶⁴

Klepper's work on *The Eternal House* was not resumed until the end of February 1942, so great had been his anxieties and time spent in contacts with publishers and correspondence with Switzerland and Sweden about Reni. Reni's twentieth birthday was celebrated on 5 March 1942. On 1 May a decree was issued forbidding Jews to use public transport unless they had to travel at least seven kilometres to get to their work.⁶⁵ As the war, especially in the east, became more problematic for Germany, German policy about not enlisting men who had non-Aryan wives began to change. Apparently, Hitler himself was now willing to have such men back in the army.⁶⁶ Also, such men, even if not re-conscripted were to be expected to be engaged in gainful employment. Two concerns, the Dietrich Reimer publishing house and an electrical factory, indicated their willingness to employ Klepper in administrative roles. The former, the publishing house, wished to help Klepper get

---

⁶¹ *Diary*, p. 983.
⁶² *Diary*, p. 985.
⁶³ *Diary*, p. 996.
⁶⁴ *Diary*, p. 997.
⁶⁵ *Diary*, p. 1056.
⁶⁶ *Diary*, p. 1063.

on with his writing.[67] Because of disorganisation at the Labour Exchange it was not until the end of July that Klepper's appointment at the Dietrich Reimer Verlag was officially confirmed. He was employed for three days a week from 8.00 am to noon.

On 18 August, Klepper noted that the deportation of Jews had once again intensified, and he named friends of Reni, and other people he knew, including an 82-year-old woman, as victims.[68] Action to try to arrange for Reni's emigration to Sweden also intensified, led by a Secretary in the Swedish Embassy in Berlin. On 13 September, Klepper heard that his former army division was involved in the fight for Stalingrad.[69] He had earlier heard about many injuries among his former comrades, including amputations of limbs because of frostbite. All this news was disturbing. Had it not been for his marriage, he would have been at Stalingrad, or perhaps even dead, by now. Had God preserved him? But if he was contemplating suicide, was this not a betrayal of God? On 28 September, his diary began with the words 'deportations. deportations – of the old and the sick; and not simply rumours, but people whom one knows'.[70]

In the second half of October, Klepper's employers, concerned for his health and wellbeing, granted him two weeks' leave, and on 15 October Klepper and Hanni set off for a visit to Würzburg, where they had been offered a room by Professor Burckheiser.[71] This holiday became a last interlude before the severe trials that lay ahead. Visits to concerts and to the main

---

[67] *Diary*, p. 1069.
[68] *Diary*, p. 1090.
[69] *Diary*, p. 1099.
[70] *Diary*, p. 1101, 'Deportationen, Deportationen – die Alten; die Kranken. Und nicht mehr Gerucht, sondern Menschen, die man kennt.'
[71] *Diary*, pp. 1105-6.

sites not yet affected by bombing, such as the cathedral and the Residenz brought a mixture of satisfaction and foreboding, as did news of house-to-house fighting in Stalingrad. On 22 October they visited Nuremberg, Hanni's birthplace, and saw places associated with her birth and upbringing. In Augsburg they were much taken with two Gothic sculptures, one of Christ blessing and the other of the risen Christ, and they purchased the former with an option on the latter. Determined to be home for Hanni's birthday on 3 November, they set back, arriving on 31 October. They were greeted in a festive way by Reni, who was able to say that Frick's protection letter had helped her to better working conditions. The sculpture of Christ blessing arrived from Augsburg on 5 November.[72]

On 24 November Klepper received notice to muster so that he and others could be assessed for appropriate duty.[73] On 28 November female Jews were informed that they must be assessed, in order to see whether those with 'privileged' marriages were in fact entitled to be privileged. The net was closing, although at his mustering on 1 December, Klepper was informed that because of his war service he should not have been required to do so. It was clear, however, that the fate of German Jewry was in its final stages.

The last six days of the Kleppers' lives began on 5 December with the exciting news that Reni would be allowed to enter Sweden.[74] It was necessary to get an exit visa for her, and Klepper wrote to Frick seeking his assistance. On 7 December a telephone call from Frick's office said that the minister would see him the following day. When they met, Frick's news was shattering. He could no longer protect either Reni or

---

[72] *Diary*, p. 1118.
[73] *Diary*, p. 1122.
[74] *Diary*, p. 1127.

Hanni. The compulsory divorce of men with non-Aryan wives was to be set in motion, after which Hanni would be deported. The only solution would be for Hanni to obtain permission to accompany Reni to Sweden. With regard to an exit visa for Reni, this could only be granted by the Security Police. Frick had no authority in the matter.

On 9 December Hanni went to the Swedish Embassy, and Klepper went to see Adolf Eichmann at the Security Ministry. Eichmann promised a decision the following day, but made it clear that a joint exit visa for Reni and Hanni was out of the question.[75] On 10 December Klepper was informed by Eichmann's office that Reni's exit visa had been refused. The family made preparations to end their lives that same evening by gas poisoning. They died together on the evening and morning of 10 and 11 December under the protection of the sculpture of Christ blessing.

A few neighbours and some friends and some members of the congregation, around 80 in all, gathered in the churchyard at Nikolassee on the morning of 15 December for the funeral.[76] Nothing was said other than the liturgy and the readings, which were: 1 Corinthians 6.19-20, ('Know ye not that your body is the temple of the Holy Ghost which is in you, which ye have of God, and ye are not your own? For ye are bought with a price'); Matthew 7.1, ('Judge not, that ye be not judged'); Ephesians 6.10-17 (the passage about putting on the whole armour of God); and Romans 8.37-39 ('In all these things we are more than conquerors through him that loved us. For I am persuaded, that neither death, nor life, nor angels, nor principalities, nor powers, nor things present, nor things to come, nor height, nor depth, nor any other creature, shall be

---

[75] *Diary*, p. 1133.
[76] K. Pagel in Klepper, *Die Flucht*, p. 5.

able to separate us from the love of God, which is in Christ Jesus our Lord').[77] The psalm was 130 and Luther's great hymn based upon it, *Aus tiefer Not*, was sung. Today a single cross marks the three graves, bearing the three names, with Jochen in the middle, Reni to his left as one faces, and Hanni to the right.

---

[77] Eva-Juliane Meschke, in *Gast und Fremdling*, who gives the details of the readings on p. 323, also cites Hebrews 5.15-16 as a passage used at the funeral, but these verses do not exist. The Lutheran burial service cites Hebrews 4.14-16 among the possible readings. They contain the words, 'We have not an high priest which cannot be touched with the feeling of our infirmities; but was in all points tempted like as we are...'

CHAPTER 2

The Christian Novelist

In December 1939, Klepper completed an article for the magazine 'Die Zeitwende', entitled 'Der christliche Roman'.[78] This was enlarged and published as a pamphlet by the Eckart publishing house the following year,[79] and appeared after his death in a collection of writings published by Eckart under the title *Nachspiel*.[80] The Eckart publishing house, established in 1933 by Kurt Ihlenfeld, drew together a group of Christian writers consisting of R. A. Schröder, Reinhold Schneider, Otto von Taube, Werner Bergengruen, Ina Seidel, Gertrud Bäumer, Martin Beheim-Schwarzbach and Siegbert Stehmann, in addition to Klepper.[81] Together they constituted a Christian presence in the artistic world of Hitler's Germany. Klepper's essay sought to articulate how he saw the work of the Christian novelist in this difficult situation. It was an intensely

---

[78] *Diary*, p. 830.
[79] *Diary*, p. 869.
[80] J. Klepper, *Nachspiel. Aufsätze des Erzählers*, Witten and Berlin: Eckart-Verlag, 1960, pp. 84-101.
[81] See B. Mascher, 'Jochen Klepper' in O. Mann (ed.), *Christliche Dichter im 20. Jahrhundert. Beiträge zur Europäischen Literatur*, Bern and Munich: Francke Verlag, 1968, p. 398. This volume also contains articles and brief biographies of Schröder, Schneider, Seidel and Bergengruen.

personal statement, strongly coloured by his Lutheran beliefs; but it shed important light on his writing, especially *Der Vater* and the unfinished work on Katharina von Bora. However, it is also interesting to read his first novel, *Der Kahn der fröhlichen Leute*, in the light of his later reflections on the Christian novel, because *Der Kahn* is the least explicitly or implicitly Christian writing of the three works.

The main argument of Klepper's article is that a Christian novel is determined not by its content (it could have a Christian theme or themes, but still not be Christian), but by the fact that it has been written by a Christian who is responsible to God in such a way that there are limits to what can be written. This does not mean that there is a limit on human creativity or even fantasy; it is the responsible way in which these are used that affects the Christian character of the work. Two examples of how Klepper views the limits of responsibility are, first, a commitment to absolute honesty in what is portrayed and, second, an avoidance of judgement. Judgement is something that must be left to God, although this does not mean that actions or thoughts that might need to be judged by God are to be omitted or whitewashed. This would violate the commitment to honesty. The avoidance of judgement comes from what is fundamental to Klepper's life, work and faith, an awareness of being simultaneously a sinner and justified by God's unmerited grace. In this condition, no-one has the right to judge others.

As Klepper's article proceeds, it becomes more explicitly Lutheran, in the sense that he feels an obligation to write in the spirit of what God has spoken in the Bible. This is more applicable to Klepper's poetry and hymn-writing than to his novels, but it is nevertheless a factor in the novels. Klepper feels that his whole existence depends on the fact that he is addressed by God and that he must respond, and that in this process he knows himself to be a sinner who is utterly dependent on God's forgiving grace. Thus, a Christian who is writing is doing so, not in order to become rich or famous (although Klepper's royalties from his first two novels did much to alleviate his desperate financial situation), but to serve the God who addresses him and sustains him.

Enough has been said about this article to enable us to consider the first of his novels, *Der Kahn der fröhlichen Leute (The Barge of the Joyful People)*.[82]

The idea for writing *Der Kahn* came from a remark from Klepper's wife Hanni. In the summer of 1932, they had visited Beuthen, and Hanni wondered if anything would come of her husband's plan to write about the depressing post-war situation of that part of the Oder region, about which he had been collecting newspaper cuttings. To his surprise, as he recorded in his diary,[83] the idea of writing *Der Kahn* came to him unexpectedly, and the experience of writing it was almost intoxicating.[84] It is tempting to speculate how far Klepper's recent marriage to Hanni and his acquisition of two young stepdaughters also played a part in the idea. The exact age of Wilhelmine Butenhof, the heroine of the novel, is never stated, except that she has not been confirmed, which suggests that she is not yet 14. Brigitte, Klepper's elder stepdaughter was aged 12 when the novel was being written; she had lost her father and had in effect been adopted by Klepper's marriage to Hanni. *Der Kahn* begins with the death of Wilhelmine's father, which leaves her an orphan. The local pastor appoints, as is the custom, a guardian, and the novel ends with

---

[82] Reference is made to the Fischer paperback reprint.
[83] *Diary*, pp. 25-6.
[84] 'Während ich nun an diesem Roman schreibe, bin ich...beinähe wie in einem Farbenrausch', *Diary*, p. 26.

Wilhelmine's adoption by the captain of the steamer CWV and his wife. It is unwise, of course, to try to press the parallels too closely; but they are not non-existent, even though the eventual outcome of Klepper's marriage to Hanni did not lead to the hopefulness with which the novel ends. That, of course, could not have been foreseen in 1932.

The novel begins, then, with the death of Wilhelmine's father, leaving her an orphan who has inherited her father's barge, the *Helene*, and some savings that had been put aside to buy a new barge. The local pastor appoints an elderly and respectable member of his congregation, August Müssigang, to be Wilhelmine's guardian. Wilhelmine's parents are not described in glowing terms. Her late mother was regarded as a slut (*Schlaupe*) and her father as a lout (*Grobian*, which can also mean a bargee). Wilhelmine herself is bad (*schlimm*) and many of the boat people wondered how such a young girl could be so bad.

In the event, Wilhelmine proves to be a resourceful and strong-willed person. She has grown up on the River Oder and barge life is the only life she knows. She is determined not to live on land or in a house, and the idea of school is anathema. She persuades her landlubber elderly guardian to join her on the *Helene*, in a business-as-usual arrangement. That business involves sailing downstream to the port of Stettin, where cargo is bid for to be delivered upstream. Like similar barges, the *Helene* has no engine and travels upstream as part of a convoy drawn by a steamship.

The *Helene* needs a crew, consisting of the helmsman and a boy, and between them they choose a lad named Fordan and a helmsman named Berthold Ohnesorge. Together, they navigate the *Helene* to Stettin. Alone on the *Helene* while the two men and the boy visit the town, Wilhelmine ponders the future. One possibility that occurs to her is to note where various barges are laid up for the winter, so that they can burgle the owners' houses; but what she really needs is to increase the size of her crew. Her guardian and helmsman have ready suggestions. Ohnesorge was not always a helmsman but, with his brother August, did a strong-man act in a circus. Müssigang, the guardian, also has a circus past, and knows a contortionist named Gura. Other acquaintances are Lattersch, a magician, and Winderlich, who has performed balancing acts. These join the crew of the *Helene*, together with an elderly Russian circus pony named Hannchen that can play tunes on bottles. The resourceful Wilhelmine organises their accommodation aboard the barge and, loaded with a cargo of coal, the *Helene* is towed in a convoy upstream.

Boat traffic on the Oder is interrupted by two seasons: low water in summer and the freezing of the river in winter. It is during the summer pause that Wilhelmine takes a walk on the banks of the Oder and sees the *Helene* from a distance. She sees that it is badly in need of repair, and on her return to the ship galvanises the crew to help with this work. She also decides to have the *Helene* painted blue (an unusual colour for a barge), and this decision has important consequences. The brother-in-law of the painter who is engaged for the work is the captain of the steamer CWV, Captain Woitschach, and through the painter the captain and his wife become aware of Wilhelmine and the *Helene*. The Woitschachs are childless, having lost a daughter in a drowning accident, and see in Wilhelmine the possibility of acquiring a daughter by adoption. They are further made aware of Wilhelmine and her crew when the latter begin to provide free entertainment shows for local people, many of them without work. A star turn is the pony Hannchen with her ability to play tunes on bells or bottles with her nose or hoof. The Woitschachs give a privileged position to the *Helene* when it comes to needing a tow from the steamer, but there is a long way to go in the story before the adoption happens. It is preceded by a serious illness on the part of Wilhelmine, brought on by the requirement that she should attend school. The thought of leaving the *Helene* and her crew is too hard for her to bear.

Sent home to Zeuthen by train in order to receive proper medical attention, Wilhelmine renews a friendship with Michel Burda, the teenage great-nephew of her guardian Müssigang. He is the son of a fish shop owner and Wilhelmine had earlier encouraged him to sell the fish by rowing out to the barges when they passed, instead of waiting for people to come to the shop. This has become a great success and Wilhelmine, in spite of her illness, joins Michel on one of his sales trips. A long-standing friend of Michel is a much older, lonely woman named Zerline, who has also had theatrical connections in earlier life. She offers the warmth and comfort of her home to Wilhelmine.

The approach of winter and the freezing of the river raise the question of what will happen to the crew of the *Helene* once she reaches Zeuthen and cannot move because of the ice. Wihelmine is determined that as many as want to should continue to live on the barge, although winter quarters will have to be found for the pony Hannchen.

Wilhelmine has another idea. Because the freezing of the river will make it no longer possible for Michel to take fish to the barges, she suggests that they should sell fish to local villages. The pony Hannchen is attached to a small cart, and the crew help in the business of selling to the villages the fish that Michel provides.

Two moments of sadness precede the happy ending of the book: the severity of the winter ice and storms damages the *Helene* badly, and the old pony Hannchen reaches the end of her life. What will the future hold as the Oder becomes navigable again? Wilhelmine and Michel have become close friends, and when she asks him whether he has plans for marriage and the future, he replies, 'Not without you'. The arrival of the steamer CWV brings Wilhelmine back into contact with Captain Woitschach and his wife, and renews their hopes of adopting her. She joyfully declares that they will not only have a daughter but a potential son-in-law. One day Wilhelmine and Michel will be Herr and Frau Kapitän of the steamer CWV.

In summarising the plot of *Der Kahn*, I have been unable to indicate the richness of the detail that it contains. According to Kurt Ihlenfeld, Klepper not only spoke with a slight Silesian accent; he also used typical Silesian diminutive forms when he spoke, such as 'Häusel' for 'Haus', 'Kindel' for 'Kind' and 'Städtel' for 'Stadt'. The dialogue in *Der Kahn* is rich with such forms, and the descriptions of the customs, the countryside and the general atmosphere of the Oder region can only have been written by someone intimately familiar with it. Yet Klepper succeeds in transporting readers into the unfamiliar world of the 1920s, so that they quickly feel at home there and empathise with the characters who live out their lives in the harsh conditions which nature imposes.

The novel is not in any way religious. At Christmas, only Wilhelmine of the crew of the *Helene* goes to the service on Christmas Eve, the main religious celebration; but there is a lovely passage at the end of the book when Wilhelmine drops in on a wedding taking place in Zeuthen:

> With dear God she felt herself completely at peace; and with what had happened: with the barge, its crew, with Michel, with the orphanage for boat-children, with the captain and his wife, with Hannchen.[85]

Otherwise, the novel is a tribute to what can be done in adversity and how good can come from what is bad. If there is no attempt at social criticism, neither is there anything political. There are also no judgements. There is no character who feels a sinner and redeemed. Indeed, it can hardly be called a Christian novel according to the criteria that Klepper later worked out. Yet one criterion was in his mind, if not in the book.

On 13 September 1933 he noted in his diary that the idea for a new book about Frederick William I had come to him, pushing aside other ideas he had been considering.[86] During the previous weekend of 9-10 September he had been visiting Potsdam and had seen in the city palace some pictures painted by the king. He would later publish some of these in *In Tormentis Pinxit*. They had given Klepper a completely new insight into the character of Frederick William, quite different from the conventional view.[87] But there was another factor in Klepper's decision to write *Der Vater*:

> Today the *Losung* refers to Isaiah 48.1-11. This must have affected me, now, if believing in the book [presumably, the Bible], that is, God's promise to support me in my work, without knowing anything about the book [presumably *Der Vater*].

---

[85] 'Aber mit dem lieben Gott fühlte sie sich ganz in reinen. Mit dem Kahn. Mit ihren Leuten. Mit Michel. Mit dem Waisenhaus für Schiffskinder. Mit Kapitäns. Mit Hannchen. *Der Kahn*, p. 197.
[86] *Diary*, p. 107.
[87] *Diary*, p. 106.

The passages quoted in the diary are as follows:

> I have declared the former things from the beginning; and they went forth out of my mouth, and I shewed them; I did them suddenly, and they came to pass (Isaiah 48.3).
> I have shewed thee new things, from this time, even hidden things, and thou didst not know them (Isaiah 48.6b).
>
> Behold, I have refined thee, but not with silver; I have chosen thee in the furnace of affliction (Isaiah 48.10).

Klepper seems to have understood this text to mean that God had given him the idea to write *Der Vater* and, if this is correct, the novel met the criterion of writing done in obedience to God's guidance, and not done for money or fame. As he began his research for the novel, the main question that the novel would address became clear to him: 'How can a Christian be a ruler? How can you rule, carrying responsibility, and build something up in the awareness of being a sinner?'[88] The last point, awareness of being a sinner, was also a responsibility before God that a Christian writer had to bear.

The novel is divided into two parts, the first of which has seven, the second of which has eight chapters. Each chapter is headed by a quotation from the Bible, without the reference being given, and the whole book is prefaced by a quotation from Frederick William, 'Kings must suffer more than other people'.[89]

The first chapter, entitled 'König Midas' ('King Midas'), begins with Frederick William, the nineteen-year-old crown prince, preparing for the baptism of his first son Frederick Ludwig. It

---

[88] *Diary*, p.116, for 22 October 1933: 'Wie kann ein Christ ein Landesvater sein? Herrschen, Verantwortung tragen, Aufbauen in Sünderbewusstsein?'
[89] 'Könige müssen mehr leiden als andere Menschen'.

is typical of Klepper's style that he appears to assume that readers are familiar with the facts of Frederick William's life and that there is no need to tell them about his birth, childhood, and marriage to Sophie Dorothea of Hanover in 1706. The narrative moves swiftly to portray the dire condition of the country ruled by the first 'King in Prussia', Frederick I. The government is dominated by the three W's, the Counts Wittgenstein, Wartenberg and Wartesleben, and the court is sufficiently bankrupt and corrupt to be tricked by a charlatan posing as Count Gaëtano, who claims to be able to turn base metals into gold. On the basis of this promise, the king has made lavish and unaffordable grants and promises to the alchemist. The crown prince learns the truth about Gaëtano from a young man named Creutz. He decides to gain experience with the army, fighting in Flanders, through which he meets, and begins a lifelong association with, Count Leopold of Ansbach-Dessau, twelve years older than himself and an accomplished military commander. News reaches Frederick William of the death of his son, and after the birth of his second child, Wilhelmine, he goes with Count Leopold to take part in the Battle of Malplaquet. Again, Klepper assumes that his readers know about this costly battle in 1709 in the context of the War of the Spanish Succession. For Klepper, what matters is how the crown prince begins to learn at first-hand what the lot of an ordinary soldier is like. We see signs of Frederick William's dislike of the privileges and comforts enjoyed by the ruling classes. On his way back to Berlin, Frederick William rests at the fortress of Küstrin, where he witnesses the execution of the by now unmasked Gaëtano.

Back in Berlin, the king has married for a third time, the unfortunate Sophie Louise of Mecklenburg-Schwerin-Grabow, so great is his anxiety to produce another male child. During the wedding festivities, the crown prince attends a function at the house of Count Grumbkow where, wearied by talk about the latest fashions in Paris, the crown prince challenges those present to follow him in throwing his wig and an ornate coat into the stove. Frederick William, Grumbkow and Leopold make a pact looking to the future of Prussia. Another son is born to the crown prince, but alas, this Frederick William lives only a year. The chapter ends on this sad note, and there is no gold. The dream of King Midas is an empty one.

The second chapter is entitled 'Der Plusmacher' ('The profit maker'), evidently a name given to Frederick William by those who found themselves on the wrong side of his far-reaching financial reforms. It begins as the crown prince begins to take over the reins of power. The old king's death is treated with great respect, and the traditional ceremonies are scrupulously observed. However, from the moment of Frederick William's inauguration as king, it is clear that a new age is dawning. His inauguration ceremony is much simplified, and the new king embarks on a series of financial reforms, in order to rescue his kingdom from the disastrous legacy left by King Midas. A master of detail, Klepper brilliantly describes the reforms: the replacement of gold and dinner services with pewter, the melting of the gold for coinage, the drastic reduction in the numbers of state officials and the lower salaries of those who remain, the reduction in the number of diplomats, the king's determination to end the import of food and materials and to make Prussia self-sufficient. We get a glimpse of Frederick William's working day beginning at 4.00 am, with the king meditating on the Bible; and we see the king's growing awareness of how weak, tiny and poor his country is, and how it is surrounded by countries that would readily dismember and absorb it. Klepper sensitively describes the relationship that then exists between Frederick William and his wife Sophie Dorothea, a bond made stronger by his wife's remarkable fertility. They share the joy of the birth of the crown prince Frederick, later Frederick II, and the sadness of the death of a third child, who lives only a year, the Princess Charlotte.

The third chapter is entitled 'Segel auf dem Wintermeer' ('Sail on the winter sea') and is entirely concerned with the siege of Stralsund and the adjacent island of Rügen. Again, Klepper gives no dates or historical background, but assumes that readers will know that parts of Pomerania, an arc of land from Stralsund to Stettin, had been Swedish territory since the end of the Thirty Years War, that Karl XII of Sweden had been defeated and exiled to the Ottoman Empire in 1709 following a campaign deep into Russian territory; and that he had escaped around 1715 and was staying in Stralsund. Fearing that this brilliant military leader would rally Sweden and again attack northern German states, an alliance was formed, but only Frederick William with his newly emerging army seems to have taken any action, by blockading and besieging Stralsund.

Klepper describes how the Prussian army, on the advice of Over-Lieutenant Koeppen, who has grown up in the area, takes advantage of a narrow sandbank which under certain conditions gives access to Stralsund. Surprising the defenders of the city, the Prussians force Karl XII to take refuge on the island of Rügen, only to be met there by overwhelming numbers of Prussian soldiers. Karl, badly wounded, escapes to Sweden. Frederick William is able to take control of territory as far as the great port of Stettin, where he is greeted as a liberator, although Stralsund is still denied to him.

An interesting incident is the arrival of the pregnant queen Sophie Dorothea in the king's camp. Frederick William goes out of his way to provide for her welfare and comfort, painfully aware of the contrast between the expenditure that this entails, and the harsh conditions endured by his troops. The chapter ends in the growing awareness that Frederick William's kingdom is beginning to assume a more solid shape that will ensure its future.

Two main incidents dominate the fourth chapter entitled 'Wirte und Gäste' ('Landlords and guests'); they are the visit of Peter the Great to Berlin in 1718, and the encounter between Frederick William and the nobility. The nobles had usually visited Berlin several times a year in the days of Frederick William's father. On the grounds of economising, this is reduced to one visit under Frederick William, and the assembled nobles find themselves in a Berlin that has been noticeably affected by the economies from the point of view of the entertainments that are offered. The nobles are also addressed by the young king and left in no doubt that times have changed, and that the king expects their estates to be administered responsibly and with due regard for the farmers and workers. Also, appropriate taxes are to be paid to the king. The nobles are shocked by this news, and the king is accused of having more concern for ordinary citizens than for the nobility. The king reminds them that when estates fall vacant because there is no proper heir, they fall to the possession of the crown. Frederick William indicates that it is in his power to take possession of such estates or to pass laws affecting inheritance, which include making it possible for daughters to inherit. The matter is not resolved by Frederick William, but he declares his intention to visit the estates and to ensure that they are being properly governed.

There is a sub-plot to this main event. The young man, Creutz, whom Frederick William has made his chief accountant, and whose work in putting the king's finances on a firm footing is succeeding, develops a fancy for a beautiful young noblewoman, Fräulein von Wagnitz. She has been cheated financially by nobles in Prussia and wants Creutz to help her to redeem her debts. Frederick William accidentally overhears her complaints, and it strengthens his resolve to visit the eastern estates. However, the noblewoman has higher aims, to become Frederick William's mistress and if possible to oust Sophie Dorothea. A rumour is spread among the assembled nobles that she is indeed the king's mistress. This attempt to undermine Frederick William's authority leads to a showdown between the king, the young woman and Creutz, who has meanwhile been promoted to the rank of Counsellor.

The visit of Peter the Great comes during his journey home from Holland to Russia. He is anxious to meet the young king who has defeated Karl XII, mindful that the Swedish king had penetrated deeply into Russian territory in the previous decade. The Russian royal party travels by boat from Charlottenburg to the palace at Monbijou where Princess Wilhelmine, aged nine, charms the visitors. At the hunting lodge in Königs Wusterhausen, Russian presents of falcons and bears are received, the two kings declare their loyalty to each other, and the Tsar says how impressed he has been with the good order and organisation of Frederick William's kingdom.

Another sub-plot concerns the deposed high officials under Frederick William's father, Gundling and Grumbkow, and their residence in an inn maintained by the landlord Koch, which is the main meeting-point for all men of influence. Although their part in the rumour about the king's mistress is not clear, it certainly brings them satisfaction.

Earlier in the chapter, Princess Wilhelmine suffers from bleeding at the mouth, an event that makes Frederick William realise how incompetent his doctors and pharmacists are and how badly maintained their equipment is. He orders their dismissal, and determines to replace them with medical scientists using only the best and latest equipment. Realising that his anxiety for his daughter is no different from the anxieties experienced by ordinary people, he expresses a determination to make medical treatment free to all of his subjects. The chapter ends as Frederick William and Peter the Great agree, 'Happy the land whose king is noble and whose rulers eat at the right times for nourishment, not for pleasure'.

Peter the Great may well have praised Frederick William for the orderliness of his realm, but Klepper describes in chapter five, 'Heerschau und Landfahrt' ('Inspection and journey'), the Prussian king's attempts to remedy the glaring deficiencies of the realm. It is a group of disparate areas with no obvious or defensible borders. Its population is small and large parts of the land are poor for agricultural purposes. Klepper describes the enlargement of Potsdam, and the building there of new houses for craftsmen, with extra provision for accommodation for soldiers. The houses are constructed according to plans drawn up by Frederick William, with tiles, not straw roofs, and other measures taken to prevent the outbreak and spread of fire. This activity at home in the new capital is followed by a long journey to the eastern parts of his dominions, the parts that give their name to the whole kingdom, Prussia.

Among the problems encountered here are the estates of the nobles, who in some cases refer to privileges claimed to have been granted by Polish or Lithuanian rulers. Frederick William has little sympathy for such nobles who, from his point of view, do nothing to improve or properly use the agricultural land, lakes and forests that they own, and who live lives of idleness dependent upon the serfs who are not properly respected. Frederick William finds that the conditions that were complained about by Fräulein von Wagnitz are richly in evidence. The king indicates that he will no longer tolerate taxes being levied on the poor to support the nobles. They will be expected to contribute to the finances of the realm and to encourage young men to become soldiers and craftsmen. New settlements are created out of scattered communities, with boundary walls and properly built houses. Their names are given by Klepper, all of them Frederick William's towns.

Klepper mentions a picture painted by Frederick William that inspired his work. It is of a family about to be evicted from their home by a landlord. The houses are poorly built, the landscape is bare and the trees are sparse. Birds fly menacingly overhead. Klepper reproduces on page 46 of *In tormentis pinxit* a picture that resembles this description, but not in all details. For example, the wife and children of the threatened family are not depicted.

Klepper makes much of the difference between Frederick William's visits to the nobles' estates, and those of his predecessors. Royal visits previously had been occasions on which lavish entertainment and accommodation were to be offered in return for favours from the king. Frederick William travels with a small retinue and does not eat with the nobles, but more often with ordinary people. If he expects gifts, they are to be in the form of taxes and manpower to build up his fragile kingdom. The only favour he offers is that the nobles should become part of a defensible and prosperous and self-sufficient country, with an army that will be respected throughout Europe.

Klepper brilliantly moves the scene from Frederick William's austere and strenuous journeys in the east to the court in Berlin. The king's absence has been taken advantage of. There is a new scandal involving Fräulein von Wagnitz, Counsellor Creutz, a goldsmith named Lieberkuhn and the daughter of the chief steward of the palace at Charlottenburg. 'When will the king return?' is the question asked anxiously by some who have something to hide or fear, and expectantly by those who desire the king's firm hand.

The chapter ends with a scene that will prepare for the next chapter. Frederick William greatly values the preaching of a Pastor Roloff, even though Roloff is Lutheran and not Reformed like the king. Roloff's fame spreads, and one day he receives a letter asking him to receive a certain Michael Clement, Baron of Rosenau, and if possible to win him from Catholicism to Protestantism. More will be heard of Clement later. However, Frederick William's return from his journeys has one bright spot. His small son Frederick is now a colour-bearer in the army. His father promotes him to captain, and arranges for a portrait of him to be executed by Antoine Pesne.

The next chapter is entitled 'Der König und der Abenteurer' ('The king and the adventurer'). It is a dark account of the intrigues that surround the king, both at home and abroad, and reveals the king's character as never before, as a man whose concept of power is such that it brings responsibility and suffering, and is not an office which can or should be exploited in the holder's own interests or that of his family and favourites, if any.

Frederick William's response to the intrigues that have festered during his absence in the east is that he must reform the judiciary and leave it to the proper administration of the law to convict and punish wrongdoers. Time-serving judges and advocates who financially milk the system are dismissed and replaced by more competent men. The king makes it a principle that no case should take longer than three months to bring to a conclusion.

At this point, Michael Clement enters the action. At a clandestine audience with the king, he hands over letters that have sinister implications. They indicate that the rulers of Vienna, Saxony, Paris and the Netherlands have no desire to see Prussia emerge as a great power in Europe. There is an international conspiracy to assassinate Frederick William and in this way to nip the threat to their interests in the bud. The king now takes precautions for his own safety and insists on personally reading all correspondence that leaves and arrives in Berlin. Clement becomes a trusted adviser. He also becomes enamoured of Fräulein von Wagnitz; and it is she who accidentally leads to Clement's exposure and downfall.

The daughter of the owner of the prestigious Koch Hotel had become pregnant at the hands of Peter the Great. She is now seriously ill, and the narrative hints at a botched abortion. A call for Pastor Roloff to visit her leads to Fräulein von Wagnitz admitting him to the sick-bed. She then accompanies the pastor back to his lodgings where Clement resides. As they enter the house a blast of wind runs through the building. Clement is burning documents and trying to clear the smoke with open windows. The Fräulein retrieves some papers that have blown away, and notices that one of them contains repeated attempts to copy the signature of Frederick William I. Appalled at this discovery, Clement has to confess that he is a fraud; that he is not a baron and that he has been forging documents, an art that he learned while being brought up in a monastery. The Fräulein wants everything to be confessed to the king, but Clement prevails upon her to let him escape, by means of another forged letter that will summon him to the Netherlands. He confesses that he has been in the pay of the court of Vienna.

However, he has not completely fooled Frederick William, whose suspicions are aroused by obtaining a letter supposedly written and signed by him but which is a forgery. He and his trusted officials begin discreet inquiries into the origins of Michael Clement. This opens a can of worms that not only includes international plotting, but conspiracies against the king among some of his nobles and officials, alarmed about his reforms and aims. There is also a brief and unsuccessful attempt to get the army to mutiny. Clement is brought back to Berlin under armed guard and put on trial, a trial which also covers some of the local conspirators. The king, who has developed a regard and even affection for Clement, refuses to interfere with the law as it is prescribed in such cases in the Holy Roman Empire, and Clement is condemned to be tortured and hanged.

Frederick William visits the condemned man, and Klepper writes one of the most moving scenes in the whole novel. On seeing the condemned man, the king says,

> Each man must drink fully the dregs of his involvement in guilt. The king is a robber, a tyrant, a usurer, an arsonist, a murderer.[90]

Clement replies that a king is more like the cherubim in the mercy seat, and that kings who murder are stewards of God's mysteries. The king rejects this. He is merely a man who

---

[90] 'Jeder muss die Tiefen der Schuld an seinem Teil bis zum Tiefsten auskosten. Ein König wird Räuber, Tyrann, Wucherer, Brandstifter, Mörder' *Der Vater*, p. 332.

measures the acres in his field, examines the produce of his workshops and supervises the supplies for his army. Clement counters that, even so, God has placed him to be a steward of his mysteries, a miracle that is obvious to anyone who cares to see. The king replies, in a moment of unusual tenderness, that if the law did not have to take its course, he would make Clement one of his most trusted officers and advisers. Clement laughs. He does not fear death, because he has discovered the one and only King worthy of that name; and he begins to speak with bitterness of those whose attitudes to the king had wounded him, beginning with Professor Gundling.

There is a positive outcome to this dark chapter on conspiracies and intrigues. The king goes secretly to the fortress and hunting lodge of Schönebeck, to the north of Berlin. Here, he begins to draft a constitution for the whole of his kingdom. The King of Prussia and Elector of Brandenburg is uniting the Mark of Brandenburg, Prussia, Cleve, Magdeburg and Pomerania in a single state with the common order. Five years of rule have convinced him of the necessity of doing what no one but he thought was possible; the intrigues against him have misfired.

But other foes stalk the king, against which he has little defence, namely, illness and death. The chapter entitled 'Die Hütte Gottes bei den Menschen' ('God's dwelling among men') is dominated by these themes. Scarcely has Frederick William begun to organize his kingdom according to his new constitution and to inform his high officials how this will affect them, than illness and death strike. First, Princess Wilhelmine is gravely ill, and then the king's second surviving son, Karl, dies, aged two. 'Why is it', the king agonises, 'that it is my sons who do not survive?' His concern for the survival of the crown prince Frederick becomes all the more serious.

Then the king himself becomes gravely ill. He finds himself in the precincts of the cathedral at Havelberg. Although he needs to rest and sleep, he drives himself to ensure the safety of his kingdom by drafting two testaments, one to his wife, the other to the crown prince. The testament to his wife, which she reads in spite of its being embargoed until after his death, gives her full power in the Regency that will come into force until the crown prince's coming of age. The testament to his son lays out what Frederick William sees as the task of a Christian ruler of his country. Its greatest asset is its people, and they are to be visited regularly throughout the land. Unjustified war is to be avoided. History shows the hand of God at work, in which his judgement against unjust rulers can be seen. To do what is right by God is not easy, but necessary.

Having spent many hours on his sick-bed, dictating and writing in his own hand, the king needs to sleep, and the cathedral bells are silenced so as not to disturb him. The news of his serious illness brings some of his notable officials and friends to Havelberg to see him. The Duke of Anhalt-Dessau is joined by Gundling and Grumbkow, all of whom are dismissed haughtily by Queen Sophie Dorothea, encouraged by the secret knowledge of her powers of Regency. They guess what has happened and begin to work out how they can undermine the Regency, if or when it comes into force. The preacher Roloff arrives; he unnerves the plotters by expressing the view that the king is not fatally ill. He is no medical doctor, but has seen many men on their death-bed; the king is not in that condition. He returns to Berlin. A physician who appears to be competent treats the king with ipecacuanha, which has a strong emetic effect. This seems to help the king and he starts to recover. Later, the king renews his determination to put medical treatment in his realm on the best possible scientific footing, backed by autopsies and the dissection of corpses.

Jochen Klepper with his wife Hanni and his stepdaughters, Renate *(seated, right)* **and Brigitte Stein** *(standing, left)*

From Evangelische Kirchengemeinde Gönningen; Klepper's Life in Pictures
www.ekggoenningen.de/klepper

A single cross marks the grave of Jochen Klepper, his wife Hanni and stepdaughter Renate Stein

Protestant churchyard, Berlin-Nikolassee

Creative Commons, Jochen Teufel, July 2006

**Katharina von Bora
(1499-1552)
Wife of Martin Luther**

Oil on wood, 1529
Workshop of Lucas Cranach the
Elder (1472-1553)

Uffizi Gallery, Florence

**Frederick William I of
Prussia (1688-1740)
King of Prussia and
Elector of Brandenburg,
1712-1740**

Oil on canvas, 1713
Samuel Theodor Gericke
(1665-1729), court painter

*Collection of the Prussian
Palaces and Gardens
Foundation Berlin-Brandenburg,
Potsdam*

On the Sunday after his recovery begins, the king orders the cathedral bells to ring for worship. From his sick bed he hears the worship. Words from Psalm 27 fill his thoughts:

> One thing have I desired of the Lord, that I will seek after; that I may dwell in the house of the Lord all the days of my life, to behold the beauty of the Lord, and to inquire in his temple. For in the time of trouble he shall hide me in his pavilion: in the secret of his tabernacle shall he hide me; he shall set me up upon a rock (vv.4-5).

On his return to Potsdam, he resolves to build a church as close as possible to his palace – God's dwelling among his people – and the words of Jesus run through his mind, 'Wist ye not that I must be about my father's business?'

The novel has reached its halfway point. Part II contains a further eight chapters, in which the emphasis switches particularly to Frederick William's relationship with his family. The children are growing up and want to become independent. Queen Sophie Dorothea feels that she has done more than her duty when it comes to bearing children. The sense of her power hinted at by the king's testament to her when he was gravely ill boosts her sense of importance. Initially, she desires to go to England, where her father has become George I. Here, she expects to receive the honour due to the Queen of Prussia. Ill health and another unwelcome pregnancy prevent this, but she does manage to leave the Prussian court for a month to visit her family in Hanover.

During her absence, the eldest daughter Wilhelmine spends more and more time with the king, who is alarmed to hear from her that her mother fills her head, and that of her children, with romantic tales of fantasy. Frederick William decides that the education of his children must be subject to closer supervision. A new governess, a Fräulein von Sansfeld, is appointed to educate Wilhelmine. The crown prince's education is reviewed. Latin is banned from his instruction in favour of German. Military history and statesmanship occupy a prominent place in the curriculum. These plans are only partly successful. The crown prince is a voracious reader and reads into the small hours of the morning, devouring books well outside the curriculum, but giving him a wide knowledge of history and culture. Also, Frederick and his elder sister increasingly spend time together, formulating their own ideas about their lives. The queen, on her return, also interferes. Klepper describes the tug-of-war between the royal parents to influence the two eldest children as follows:

> The father was the one forever warning, relentlessly urging and ordering; the mother opposed him as the one daily sending gifts, praise, promises. The father aimed at the instruction of Prussian commanders and administrators; the mother offered beautiful romance, telling about the great world of royalty.[91]

The queen begins to plan the future for her two eldest children. Wilhelmine should marry a future heir to the English throne and become Queen of England; Frederick should marry an English princess. A visit to Berlin is arranged for George I while on a visit to the Electorate of Hanover. Wilhelmine is presented to him, but his only reaction is to remark that she is tall, and to ask her age. The English king is taken ill, and the visit is not a success. On his death in 1727, Sophie Dorothea's brother becomes George II. Hopes for a Prussian-English alliance through marriage are alive.

---

[91] *Der Vater*, pp. 437-8, 'Der Vater war der ewig Warnende, der unablässig Fordernde, Gebietende; die Mutter begegnete ihn als die tagtäglich Schenkende, Lokkende, Verheissende. Der Vater vereidigte auf die Instruktion eines preussischen Militärs und Beamten; die Mutter steckte ihm den schönen Roman zu, der von der Grossen Welt der Könige erzählte.'

The scene shifts back to Potsdam, where Frederick William initiates a new phase of turning the swampy surroundings into firm ground by filling the swamps with wooden poles. New quarters are built for craftsmen and craftswomen, new housing for the army. New methods of recruitment are instituted to expand the army.

Frederick William continues to be worried about his eastern possessions, their sparse population and poor agricultural conditions. All money that is saved by the efforts of Chancellor Creutz, the controller of the finances, is channelled to improving conditions in the east. The king also consults with Pastor Roloff about improving the education of children in the east, including their religious instruction.

This chapter is entitled 'Die aufgehende Sonne' ('The rising sun') and Klepper creates the impression that the oppositions of the past have now been overcome. Those reconciled with the army and employed in manufacturing begin to feel a sense of pride in their occupations.

The chapter closes with what Klepper surely must have intended as an implicit criticism of the regime under which he lived. On the infamous day of Potsdam, 21 March 1933, the ceremonial granting of power to Adolf Hitler by President Hindenburg had taken place in the Garrison Church in Potsdam. Klepper describes how this church is built by Frederick William, how its bells ring out a Lutheran chorale each day at midday, how the church is intended not to celebrate the military strength of Prussia, but to be a place where the army can come before God in penitence to hear God's word. It is to be a symbol of a city 'with foundations whose builder and maker is God' (Hebrews 11.10).

If readers think that Frederick William has overcome the worst crisis of his reign, Klepper disappoints them with another dark chapter, and one that leads up to an unsuccessful attempt on the part of the crown prince to break free from his father and to go his own way. The king's problems now become increasingly bound up with his own family.

Le roman comique was a satire written by the seventeenth-century French writer Paul Scarron. It is procured for the two eldest children by Sophie Dorothea, and they quickly identify its characters with leading members of the royal court. Frederick William is identified with a character named Ragotin, a kind of buffoon with a sharp and irascible temper. Klepper seems to expect readers to know this background, because without explanation he entitles the next chapter 'König Ragotins Schloss' ('King Ragotin's Castle'). The castle in question is the king's autumn hunting-lodge at Königs Wusterhausen to the south-east of Berlin. Here, the king has built some houses and a church to supplement the simple and sparse facilities of the castle.

King Ragotin's Castle occupies an important place in this chapter, at the beginning and the end. In between, there is an episode in which Frederick William's court visits the court of the Duke of Saxony and King of Poland in Dresden. The contrast between the generous and royal hospitality on display in Dresden and the austere and penurious living conditions available at Königs Wusterhausen are the cause of the severe discontent of Frederick William's family, especially that of his eldest children; but if the king's children mock their father by calling him King Ragotin, it is not clear that Klepper agrees with them. The king's extreme thriftiness is derived from his sense of responsibility to his people, especially those in the east; and there is more than a hint of guilt that in having spent so much money on the building projects in Potsdam, the king has been too concerned with his own prestige at the expense of his people.

In the first main episode centred upon King Ragotin's Castle, Frederick William invites J. A. Freylinghausen, a leading Pietist from Halle. Klepper later published Freylinghausen's account of his visit to the king in *The King and the Quiet in the Land*. The visit took place in the autumn of 1727. In the novel, Klepper portrays a king anxious to be guided by the formidable Pietist in matters of religion and conduct. Is it wrong for a Christian king to hunt and to smoke? Sophie Dorothea wants to know whether it is wrong to play cards. What might seem to modern readers to be the almost pathological concern of the king to live with his conscience could well have been intended by Klepper to point up the difference between the subject of his novel and the rulers of the Germany of his day. To want to know God's will in small matters of detail was as far removed as possible from the ideology of the National Socialist state. It must also be remembered that Klepper would be the victim of Hitler's own grandiose building plans for Berlin. One consequence of the visit of the Pietist is that Christmas is celebrated without the usual folk customs surrounding Knecht Ruprecht and the Three Holy Kings. These are religious tomfoolery. The austere puritanism (if it can be called that) spreads from Königs Wusterhausen to Berlin and Potsdam, and then throughout the land. Billiards and coffee houses are forbidden, while in churches all unnecessary monuments, hangings and decorations are removed.

An invitation for the court to visit Augustus the Strong, Duke of Saxony and King of Poland, in Dresden, reaches Berlin. The reputation of Frederick William, the 'beggar king', has travelled far and wide, the rumour being spread by his wife and eldest children, amongst others. Such a ruler makes other rulers feel uneasy, as it threatens their somewhat different ideas of how a ruler should govern subjects. The result of the visit is to widen the rift between Frederick William and his queen and eldest children. Their honoured treatment as royal personages, and the lavishness of the food provided only emphasise even more the spartan, dismal life offered to royal-born people in Prussia, especially at Königs Wusterhausen. Frederick William, however, does not miss the opportunity to ask his host embarrassing questions. How do the lavish celebrations in Dresden benefit the ordinary people? Do they bring visitors and thus new money to the realm, thereby spreading the wealth and benefiting from the goods produced by the skilled workers? Or do the festivities fall as a burden on the people who have to finance them?

Frederick William's son Frederick, crown prince of Prussia and nephew of the King of England, is especially attracted by what the royal court at Dresden offers; and it strengthens his resolve to go his own way. His father, however, embarks on a new inspection of his eastern territories, taking his son with him. They stay, not in the grand houses of the nobility of the eastern regions, but in the guest houses of peasant villages, eating the simple food offered by their hosts. On returning to Berlin, the crown prince seeks refuge in his mother's palace at Monbijou, where she has attempted to create a royal atmosphere closer to that of Dresden than to Königs Wusterhausen. But the year draws on; autumn approaches and this means that the whole court must move once again to the cramped and hated castle of King Ragotin. Here, the final scene of the chapter is played out. Its climax is an outburst by the young teenage princess, Friederike Luise. Asked by her father how she would organize her house when she was married, she replies that when she is married she will maintain a much better table – that is, meals and menus – than her father provides; and that if she has children she will not force them to eat the coarse and badly cooked food that he forces his own children to eat. The king tries to contain his temper, but loses the battle, and vents his anger by throwing plates at Frederick and Wilhelmine.

This sets the tone for the growing dissent in the royal family during the autumn in Königs Wusterhausen. The king communicates with his son, living under the same roof, by writing letters. Wilhelmine is ill, or feigns illness. The king himself begins to suffer from gout. Wilhelmine compares Königs Wusterhausen with hell, with its river being the river of death, Styx. The queen produces another son, but this is not the occasion for the joy and thanksgiving that normally accompany the birth of a royal prince.

Relationships between the courts of Prussia and England break down to the point where George II seems minded to discipline the King of Prussia by military means. The dispatch of a formidable Prussian army to the river Elbe dissuades him; but Frederick and Wilhelmine are appalled at the idea of fighting their own relatives, and the crown prince describes the uniform he is obliged to wear as a 'shroud'. The chapter ends with the introduction of a person who will shortly feature prominently in the novel, a Lieutenant Katte, who quickly becomes the confidant of the restless crown prince.

One might have expected the birth of another prince, Prince Ferdinand, to have brought joy to the king and his family, but this is not so. The chapter is entitled 'Das Kind der Schmerzen oder die Galeere' ('The child of pain or the galley') and shows the royal family becoming ever more dysfunctional. It was the queen's fourteenth pregnancy, and she has grown weary of child-bearing, especially when it no longer results in the affection of her husband, as earlier births had done. Her two eldest children no longer respect her and only seem to care for the fact that she is related to the English court, on which their own hopes are still pinned. The other children are also becoming troublesome to the point where the king considers splitting them up and assigning them to live in some of the castles at his disposal.

Klepper paints a vivid portrait of these antagonising relationships. The king is isolated, hated by his family, disliked by those who have to carry out the unremitting demands made upon the army and the craft workshops, and plotted against by other royal houses that fear his emerging power. The prince whose birth should bring joy arrives in a family rent apart by hatred. He is a child of pain. At the same time, those who have to bend unwillingly to the will of the father are likened to slaves in a galley.

Klepper brilliantly leads his readers to what will be the climax of the next part of the novel, the desertion of the crown prince and its consequences. Frederick's new companion, Lieutenant Katte, increasingly urges the crown prince to break free from his father and begins to make plans for this to occur. However, Klepper does not describe the actual attempt of Frederick to go his own way. In the absence of the king from Berlin on his forty-second birthday, Sophie Dorothea organises a party in his honour. It comes to an untimely end when the queen receives a letter from her absent husband. It confirms what rumours had predicted, that the crown prince was to make a bid for freedom. It informs her that the attempt has failed, that the crown prince has forfeited his claim to be Frederick

William's son, and that his behaviour has brought shame on the whole of the royal family.

Geldern is a small town near the border with the Netherlands, some miles roughly north of Krefeld. In Frederick William's time, it was part of the Duchy of Cleve, and thus part of Prussia. Klepper begins here what is the most powerful chapter in the novel, entitled 'Der Gott von Geldern' ('The God of Geldern'). The king, beginning his long journey back to Berlin, goes to Sunday morning service in the Protestant church in Geldern, and sees there what is called a 'mercy seat'. It is an art-work which portrays God the Father, in whose arms rests the crucified body of his Son. Frederick William demands to know what this relic of Catholic piety is doing in a Protestant church in his realm; but at the same time he is deeply moved by what he sees and how it relates to his present situation as a father with an estranged and disobedient son. He is puzzled, and his prayers and Bible meditations do not help to clear his mind.

The king's return to Berlin is awaited with fear and trembling, especially by the queen and Princess Wilhelmine. Lieutenant Katte's papers have been confiscated and are being examined. Will they contain communications between the royal women and the disgraced officer that will incriminate them in the conspiracy to assist the crown prince's rebellion? Their worst fears initially seem to be realized. Wilhelmine kneels before her father asking for his mercy, only to be struck on the face. But the king is more concerned about what to do with his son than with his wife and daughter. He seeks advice from Pastor Roloff, now a sick man. He wishes to have the concept of predestination explained to him, not by a Calvinist, but by a Lutheran.

A court martial is set up by the king at Schloss Köpenick to try the crown prince, Katte and others involved in the conspiracy. Katte is sentenced to death and others are given appropriate sentences; but the court refuses to give a verdict in the case of Frederick. True, he is a deserting officer; but he is also the king's son, and any sentence must lie with the king alone. In vain does Frederick William try to change the court's mind. He alone must decide.

Klepper describes the king's agony thus. His crown has become a crown of thorns, his sceptre a cross. God has passed judgement on the king's rule through his son's disobedience. Things are not helped by Professor Gundling's brother, who points to the work of the Halle professor of philosophy, Christian Wolff. According to Gundling's brother, Wolff has demonstrated that God is enmeshed in the laws that govern the universe, and unable to intervene or change anything. This brings no comfort to the king and leads to Wolff's dismissal from his university post.

The king pays special attention to passages in the Bible that deal with fathers and sons. The readiness of Abraham to sacrifice Isaac and its interpretation in the Letter to the Hebrews is especially significant:

> By faith Abraham... offered up Isaac... accounting that God was able to raise him up, even from the dead (Hebrews 11.17, 19).

Gradually, the king comes to the conclusion that God does not want him to offer up his son as a sacrifice to the law. God has sent Frederick after the deaths of the first two sons to be the king's heir in a kingdom entrusted to Frederick William by God. The last words spoken to the king by Pastor Roloff before the pastor's death strike home:

> There hath no temptation taken you but such as is common to man: but God is faithful, who will not suffer you to be tempted above that ye are able; but will with the temptation also make a way to escape, that ye may be able to bear it (1 Corinthians 10.13).

Frederick William decides to punish his son not by execution, but by imprisonment in the fortress of Küstrin, where he is also obliged to witness the execution of his friend Lieutenant Katte. Frederick's incarceration is relieved by books and letters smuggled to him especially through the initiative of his sister Wilhelmine. So far as the king is concerned, his son is as good as dead, but this attitude does not last. God has, as it were, raised him from the dead and a new life will begin.

Now that this crisis is over the king turns to the ever-pressing task of securing his scattered and poor land for the future, and this includes Frederick. He encourages young peasant women to be instructed in household skills, and promises them presents on their wedding days. They are the shepherdesses of the title of the next chapter ('Die Hirtinnen'). He must also deal with the pressing matter of the marriage of his eldest daughters. The plans of Sophie Dorothea for the English connections must be abandoned, so that dynastic links can be forged with neighbouring noble families. His second eldest daughter, Friederike Luise, is the first to be married, at the age of 15, to Duke Karl of Brandenburg-Ansbach. This is followed, in 1731, by the marriage of Wilhelmine, not to the Prince of Wales, but to Prince Friedrich von Bayreuth. The following year, the crown prince is married, not to an English princess, but to Elisabeth Christine of Braunschweig-Bevern.

The basic statement of these facts in no way does justice to Klepper's treatment of the diplomatic manoeuvres, female heart-searching, disappointed hopes and reluctant obedience to Frederick William's will that they imply. Of these, the disappointed hopes of Sophie Dorothea and Wilhelmine are the greatest. Indeed of becoming a queen, Wilhelmine will be a marchioness, a relatively minor figure in the royal pecking order. The consolation is that her submission to her father's will helps to open the way for Frederick William to become reconciled to the crown prince. On the king's forty-third birthday he travels to Küstrin to meet Frederick, in order to begin the process of his rehabilitation. Frederick's reluctant willingness to marry Elisabeth Christine is a sign of his submission.

For the occasion of the marriages, the prudent thriftiness of the Prussian court is somewhat relaxed. The king even gives a ball for invited guests on the occasion of Wilhelmine's wedding, but not before he has satisfied himself that his daughter can recite the Creed and the Lord's Prayer.

The chapter ends on a high note. The persecution of Protestants in the region of Salzburg produces a wave of refugees. They are not only invited to Prussia by Frederick William, they are ceremonially and officially welcomed. Houses, churches and schools will be provided for them in the eastern territories. The cost is unimportant; the land needs to be occupied. The newcomers arrive singing hymns, the east is a modern Canaan. The king's thoughts are filled with God's promises to create a land and a people.

The king is on his travels in the next chapter, not to see his eastern territories, but to visit the Holy Roman Emperor in Vienna. He wants to make known his view that while he has no objection to the emperor being succeeded by his daughter, he would object to her being married to anyone other than a German. The emperor receives him as Elector of Brandenburg, rather than as King of Prussia. On his way home, Frederick

William visits Wilhelmine, whose Bayreuth marriage has turned out badly, with her father-in-law wasting the money she brought with her into the marriage. To greet her father she furnishes rooms with deliberate simplicity, gaining an appreciation that moves to a touching scene between father and daughter. They are visited by the younger daughter Friederike Luise, whose Ansbach marriage has likewise not turned out well. Frederick William is filled with guilt.

Back in Berlin, a Dr Fassmann has arrived, who has shown the work of Professor Gundling to be full of errors. A duel between the two men has led to the embarrassment for Gundling of his wig being shot off. The king wishes to know more about Gundling's errors, and this leads to his dismissal of Gundling as president of the Scientific Academy. However, Dr Fassmann, who has written among other things a book entitled *Conversations from the World of the Dead*, in which there are imaginary conversations between great figures of the past, declines to fill Gundling's position, and leaves Berlin. He is replaced by Jakob Morgenstern.

The king asks Morgenstern to organize a colloquium at the University of Frankfurt an der Oder, on the subject of folly and the position of fools and naves. The king feels that up to now he has been surrounded by such people, including Gundling. There are two outcomes. First, the king is induced to read for himself the works of the philosopher Christian Wolff, whom he had earlier dismissed from the University of Halle on the basis of excerpts from his writings supplied by Professor Gundling's brother. The king is much impressed, and resolves to reinstate Wolff. The latter is unwilling to leave Marburg where he now teaches, but the king becomes a close student of his philosophy.

This has a second consequence. The king becomes convinced of the importance of secular learning, and orders the universities in Prussia to be properly financed, and for its teaching staff to be appointed from the best scholars available. A kind of Staff College for officers is established in Potsdam. Henceforth, the king will have not only a finely trained and equipped army, but also an educated one.

This expenditure brings the king into conflict with his financial controller Creutz, who cannot see the point of expenditure on education. Further, Creutz's desire to marry his daughter, who is now very rich, to someone not closely involved in Prussian affairs, angers the king. As a result of this confrontation, Creutz takes his own life. Among his papers is found not only a great deal of money, but also evidence that he had been involved in intrigues against the king.

The King of France decides to march against the emperor in Vienna and both sides seek Frederick William's support. The king remains loyal to Vienna and promises, as Elector of Brandenburg, to contribute 14,000 men for the emperor's army. Hostilities do not break out, but the arrival of the Prussian contingent in the allied camp causes a sensation. The extremely tall Prussian soldiers, dressed in fine uniforms with magnificent equipment, bring with them a cavalry of magnificent horses, bred in the east in the tradition of the Templar Knights, who settled in the eastern frontiers several centuries earlier. Not only does the quality of the Prussian troops amaze the other generals, but instead of living with them in the luxury of a local palace, Frederick William, with his son, now a major-general at his side, has a camp close to his army which he visits regularly. If there is no fighting, the Prussian army nevertheless wins an important victory in the respect it gains.

The sojourn in the camp brings illness upon the king, now aged forty-three. He is taken to nearby Holland for treatment, and brings back with him a sarcophagus which he had ordered in case he died. He recovers, but his thoughts begin to turn to his death. Back in Berlin he receives a present from Dr Fassmann, the author of the *Conversations from the World of the Dead*. The book is about the achievements and laws of Frederick William I. He will go down in history!

The death of Creutz reveals that the kingdom is richer than supposed. This leads to a relaxation of the austerity that has marked Frederick William's reign. Even the royal palaces are allowed to start being furnished in a matter befitting royalty. More churches and houses are built, and a theatre is opened in Berlin. Ordinary citizens and soldiers are given presents and rewards for their services. Best of all, from Frederick William's point of view, he is able to give Schloss Rheinsberg to the crown prince and his daughter-in-law, and to allow them to spend money on its furnishings. In turn, the royal couple are able to invite the king and queen to enjoy their hospitality. The royal family begins to grow closer. Frederick William and his son receive Holy Communion together, the younger sons have an enthusiasm for the army, and the king hopes to arrange for his unmarried daughters to be happier than Wilhelmine.

Yet there is a note of melancholy. Being a king is burdensome. The king has to sin and to suffer more than ordinary people, and Frederick William wishes that Prussia was a republic. He purchases a house in Holland in Hoenslardyck and enjoys staying there in the anonymity of being 'Mijnheer von Hoenslardyck', which is the title of the last-but-one chapter. Tired and unwell as his life comes to an end, he renews his interest in painting and spends as much time doing this as possible – *in tormentis pinxit*.

In the final chapter, Klepper movingly portrays the last days of the king who, suffering from gout and dropsy, and looking to his son like a man a hundred years old, has to be transported in a wheelchair to review his troops and to attend church. The chapter abounds in references to the Bible as the king discusses his approaching death. An alarming factor is that the crown prince becomes ill, and after recuperating and returning to Rheinsberg, discovers that his palace is being destroyed by fire, and that his wife is arranging for its evacuation.[92] The title of this last chapter is 'Der Spiegel' ('The mirror'). On his deathbed, the king asks for a mirror in which to look at himself. This reminds him of the passage in 1 Corinthians 13:

> For now we see through a glass, darkly; but then face to face: now I know in part; but then shall I know even as also I am known (v.12)

In his first novel, Klepper takes his readers to the unfamiliar world of the barge traders of the River Oder of the 1920s. In *Der Vater* he takes them to a Prussia quite different from the Prussia that was familiar to his first readers in the 1930s. Yet if it was a different Prussia in the sense that it was merely an association of territories scattered from west to east, one thing had not changed, and that was human nature. The Prussia described in *Der Vater* is inhabited at the noble level by people who enjoy the privileges of high birth, whose lives are driven by ambition and intrigue, corruption and unfaithfulness. This Prussia is not dissimilar to the Germany of Klepper's day, where high party officials enjoyed special privileges and were constantly jockeying against each other for higher power and influence.

---

[92] Klepper wrote an account of this, which can be read in *Nachspiel*, 'Rheinbergs letzte Nacht', pp. 7-19.

I have said that Klepper describes a Prussia where human nature has not changed; but that Prussia is confronted in the novel by an alternative vision of what it means to be human, the vision that drives and shapes Frederick William. True, the king displays characteristics that are typical of human nature. He is short-tempered and irritable; he is domineering. But he also represents another world, that of faith. Indeed, it is not going too far to say that in Klepper's interpretation, Frederick William's view of kingship owes much to the Old Testament concept of the king as the shepherd of his people, responsible to God for their welfare.

Each of the fifteen chapters in *Der Vater* is headed by a quotation from the Bible with no reference being given. In every case, the quotation is from the Old Testament. In one way this is not surprising, because the political situation of the Old Testament is quite different from that in the New Testament, where the Jews no longer have a king. But Klepper's references to the Old Testament have to be set against the fact that movements within the Church, and certainly within the state at the time when Klepper was writing, were hostile to the Old Testament as a 'Jewish' composition. Luther was condemned for having translated the Old Testament into German, and attempts were being made to revise the order of worship in churches, so that the 'Jewish' elements, including the Old Testament, were removed.[93]

References to the Old Testament, then, were a provocation; but *Der Vater* contains a much more constant critique of the National Socialist regime. If it is correct to say that the Prussia described by Klepper is similar in regard to ambitious human

---

[93] See most recently J. Wallmann, 'Ein Vermächtnis Kaiser Wilhelm II. Was hat Walter Grundmanns Eisenacher "Entjudungsinstitut" mit Martin Luther zu tun?', in *Zeitschrift für Theologie und Kirche* 114 (2017) pp. 289-314.

nature to the Germany of his day, it is also correct to say that that Prussia is confronted by a biblical view of what society should be like, as embodied in the person of Frederick William. As I have said, Frederick William is not presented by Klepper as faultless, or as a saint. On the contrary, his faults are fully on display. But for all his failings, Frederick William is a man who trusts in God and who believes that his kingship has been entrusted to him by God. He is fully aware that he is a sinner who constantly stands in need of God's mercy. For this reason, the king must suffer more than other people.

Judged by the criteria mentioned at the beginning of this chapter in Klepper's article on the nature of Christian writing, *Der Vater* meets the demands fully. No-one is judged. Everything is described honestly. There is no overt preaching or proselytising. The theme is not overtly Christian. Yet the result is something that is profoundly Christian in the way that Klepper describes a corrupt and selfish society, confronted by a flawed and tyrannical ruler, who is nonetheless a means of grace to his scattered and impoverished land and people, a father to the land and people, because he is utterly dependent upon God.

Klepper's third novel, entitled *Das ewige Haus* (*The Eternal House*), was not completed. Although his literary remains contain an outline of the whole novel, with all the prospective chapter headings and, in the case of some chapters, extensive notes and summaries, only the text of the opening chapter, setting the scene for the escape of the nine nuns on Easter Eve, was completed. There is no indication of how the completed novel might have looked, and how, or whether, it would have met Klepper's criteria to be a Christian writing. However, in *Der Vater* we have not only a sufficient, but an impressive, testimony to the view that Klepper is a major Christian writer.

CHAPTER 3

Poet and Hymn Writer

At about the same time that he published an essay on the Christian novel, Klepper published an essay on Christian hymnology.[94] The criteria that he proposed were few. First, Christian hymns should be saturated with biblical language, by which Klepper meant the language of Luther's translation of the Bible. Second, the hymns should try to imitate biblical passages poetically, many of which are eminently suitable for such treatment. As an example he gives the following words from Isaiah 50.4:

> The Lord GOD hath given me the tongue of the learned, that I should know how to speak a word in season to him that is weary: he wakeneth morning by morning, he wakeneth mine ear to hear as the learned.

These words, indeed, became the basis for one of Klepper's hymns. At this point, we encounter the difficulty for English readers that Klepper's poetry is almost impossible to translate. It is characterised by simplicity of language, rhyme and metre

---

[94] 'Das göttliche Wort und der menschliche Lobgesang' in *Nachspiel*, pp. 102-131.

which cannot be reproduced in English. The following attempt to do justice to Klepper's 'Morgenlied' ('Morning Song'), prefaced by Isaiah 50.4b, 5, 8, is bound to be inadequate, as will all the other translations:

> He wakes me every morning,
> himself he wakes my ear.
> God does not remain hidden
> but leads me to the day
> in order that with his own Word
> I greet the morning light.
> He stands at dawn's own portal,
> is close to me and speaks.
>
> He speaks as on the very day
> that he the world did make.
> Silenced are fear and bitterness,
> his call alone has worth.
> The word of endless loyalty
> that God to mankind swears
> I feel in all its newness,
> as a disciple hears.
>
> He wishes me to join him,
> I do not turn my back.
> In him is my delight
> and in his Word my luck.
> I shall not be ashamed
> when only him I trust.
> God frees me from the fetters,
> God makes me be at home.
>
> He daily is so near me,
> himself declares me just.
> What I from him as gift receive
> comes not from Lord to slave.
> How lucky here the servant!
> The master is prepared
> to wake him from his slumber,
> his service to engage.

> Right early he surrounds me
> with his own Word and light,
> to promise and to realise
> that nothing will me blight,
> will fully pay my wages,
> not ask me if I will.
> His Word will shine in brightness
> However dark the day.[95]

This is one of several hymns that are found today in the *Evangelisches Gesangbuch* (Number 452).

The collection, entitled *Kyrie,* which the Eckart Verlag published in 1938, contains 29 hymns, of which six are connected with Christmas, and the remainder, having covered morning and evening, go through the Church's year, concluding with hymns for birth, baptism, confirmation, marriage and Holy Communion. Each one is preceded by an unreferenced quotation from the Bible, with the exception of the Ambrosian morning song, based upon Ambrose's Latin hymn, 'Iam lucis orto sidere'. Fifteen of the quotations come from the Old Testament.

Looking back over the 'Morning Song' we see that Klepper has not only versified the quotation from Isaiah chapter 50. He has combined it with thoughts from 2 Corinthians 4.6 and Genesis 1.2. Thus, there is a link back to the creation of the world, with the word spoken at dawn to the poet being the same word that brought the world into being:

> He speaks as on the very day
> that he the world did make.

---

[95] *Kyrie*, pp. 9-10, *Ziel der Zeit*, pp. 46-7.

Another interpretative point prominent in Klepper's Lutheran theology is that God's word is a word that justifies the ungodly, thus:

> Himself declares me just.

The poem that begins from verses in Isaiah 50 broadens out to embrace creation, redemption, God's creative and justifying Word, God's continual upholding presence through his Word and faithful promises.

Christmas was probably the festival that was most precious to Klepper, and thus it is no accident that there are five hymns dealing with Christmas. The first of the Christmas songs is prefaced by biblical verses from Hebrews 1.1-3 and 1 John 3.2; yet Philippians 5.2-9 must surely also have been in Klepper's mind.

> Who were you, Lord, before this night?
> One to whom heavenly praise was made.
> You were with God before all time,
> you were the very ray of Glory.
> All that lived was contained in you,
> All creation by you made.
> You were very God before this night.
>
> Who was I, Lord, before this night?
> One mired in shame and grief!
> For I was flesh and quite corrupt,
> lost, disinherited from hope,
> extinguished was I from all light,
> before the judgement stood condemned.
> I, object of God's love and grace,
> was darkness, death and night.
>
> Who did you become, Lord, on this night?
> You with whom the angels laughed,
> who nothing lacked of praise and honour,
> chose to bear my punishment,

> became a child in manger poor,
> atoned for mankind's dismal fall.
> You, Lord, in your highest heavenly pomp
> became companion of my very night.
>
> Who did I become, Lord, on this night?
> Be still, my heart, and only gently beat!
> Through God's own Son his son I was.
> God thought of me as his own son.
> I know not yet what I shall be,
> I sense no more than a bright glimpse.
> This you have stirred up, Lord, this night,
> at your poor stall this holy night.[96]

Klepper never thought of the birth of Jesus apart from his redeeming death, and this thought comes out clearly in this poem. An interesting thought comes in the third verse:

> You, Lord, in your highest heavenly pomp
> became companion of my very night.

There seems to be no hint here of the so-called 'kenosis' theology based upon an interpretation of Philippians 2.8, 'He humbled himself', where the Greek *ekénôsen* can be translated 'he emptied himself'. Klepper's thought seems to be paradoxical here. The one who becomes the child of the poor stall does so in his full heavenly pomp.

Sleeplessness was a problem that often plagued Klepper. Ironically, it was solved during his months of military service! No doubt the change of circumstances and the advantages of a more active life in the open air had something to do with it. The worry that everyday life, apart from his time in the army, must have brought upon him cannot have helped if he had a tendency to sleeplessness. In the light of this, his 'Song of

---

[96] *Kyrie*, pp. 24-5, *Ziel der Zeit*, pp. 56-7.

Comfort in the Evening' is all the more striking. It is prefaced by Jeremiah 15.16:

Thy word is my heart's joy and consolation.

On every night that brings a threat
your star has always risen,
and following, Lord, your stern command
your angels come to serve me.
Whatever perils me surround
your strong word you to me have sent.

If anxious doubt has me assailed
the truth from me has not removed.
Your great heart has not reckoned up
how often I betray myself and you.
You knew so well what brings me down.
Your word remained: let there be light!

If heavy woes have me oppressed,
your faithfulness to me was promised.
The stumbling-one you guided well,
will always pull him from disaster's brink.
Whenever the path I did not see,
your word did show me. The goal was near.

If my sins have me accused,
already spoken is your pardoning word.
What judge has ever thus-wise pledged
his loyalty to the guilty?
Whatever I have brought upon myself,
your word has concerned my salvation.

In every night that me surrounds,
into your arms I may collapse.
And you, who think of nought but love,
watch over me; watch over all.
You shield me in the darkness.
Your Word is faithful unto death itself.[97]

---

[97] *Kyrie*, pp. 19-20, *Ziel der Zeit*, p. 53.

I have already mentioned the Olympic Sonnets and the Kings' Poems. Of the latter, the second poem is perhaps the most profound. It is prefaced by a quotation that for once is given a reference, Proverbs 20.28:

> *Mercy and truth preserve the king:*
> *and his throne is upholden by mercy.*

Soon will a thousand years be gone
and God's new hour will break in.
Will then the king his throne ascend
and order reign throughout the world?

Then while they wait for the new thousand years,
the 'still in the land' wait anxiously,
because for the king they have waited too long,
those who seek, Lord, the kingdom only you desire.

The nations stand in weapons locked,
valuing the one who new ways of death can devise;
and when their sickles into swords they make,
their destruction is thereby decreed.

That thus deluded they continue to destroy,
is the greatest folly of this world.
He must come, who the Cross will raise
and place this sign over all.

The world by weapons is enfeebled,
and many see their power as deceit.
The king whose gaze is fixed upon the Cross
alone is he who can come to bring us aid.

Only he who from afar the Cross does see
can understand its holiness in earthly judgement.
If kings do not find your Golgotha,
their thrones they also will not find.[98]

---

[98] *Ziel der Zeit*, p. 40

The final poem that I want to try to translate is entitled 'John 15.3' and carries that text:

Now ye are clean through the word
which I have spoken unto you.

It is fulfilled, God, brought about by you.
You have brought us to the goal of time,
for in your Son have I been made your child.
Although in sin and denial still I live,
of works counts only your own work in me.
In word, only the Word from you creates.
I desired to flee, but you, Lord, were on watch.

Further life can be nought but dying,
the hours pass, however, not in vain.
I wander from the world to come to you,
deserting now my part in life to play.
Hourly pile up the burdens of all sins,
yet through the word that you have spoken
and because of it, am I clean.

Now know I that righteousness that comes with your word.
What can I yet experience from the world?
tired of being human – yet God's image.
Help me in this faith, Lord, keep me safe.
Earthly time and its guilt sink down.
You are he who both commands and fulfils.
What cannot be completed you alone complete!

So come, dear day of judgement. Pass away, final night.
And if I thither go through suffering,
your wisdom has already foreordained
that underneath the Cross I first shall understand.
Only 'neath the Cross to your Son am I near,
only where your Son is, are you, Father, there.
It is fulfilled, God, brought about by you.[99]

---

[99] *Ziel der Zeit*, p. 27.

This poem was sent to Klepper's friends the Meschkes on 29 October 1937, but without any explanation.[100] Neither is any light thrown on the circumstances by his diary. In both the letter and the diary entries for that period, Klepper bemoans the way in which the Reformation anniversary (31 October) is being played down. Also, he laments the difficulty of finding a church to attend that meets his needs. Perhaps the poem was meant to compensate for how he felt. However, whatever the reasons Klepper had for composing it, it remains a remarkable piece in its own right. It expresses Klepper's faith in strongly Lutheran terms, especially in the final words, where the thought moves from the Cross, to the Son, and the Father, the one who completes what cannot be completed, including the salvation, the ultimate making whole, of transient and sinful humanity. When I first came across a verse of a hymn from Klepper in *Die Losungen* and discovered that it had been written in 1938, I wondered how anybody could be writing such things at that awful time. I now see the answer. It came from Klepper's trust in God.

Taken as a whole, Klepper's hymns and poems are a powerful indication of his inner hope in God's purposes and guidance, despite all the attendant problems of life. How that hope was sustained through his study of the *Losungen* is the subject of the next chapter.

---

[100] *Gast und Fremdling*, pp. 96-8.

CHAPTER 4

Living in God's World as in Scripture

The *Losungen* of the Moravian Brotherhood are chosen in the following way. In a tray are 1,824 passages from the Old Testament, written on folded pieces of paper. The presiding person chooses one at random. To this is then added an appropriate New Testament text and an appropriate verse from a hymn, prayer or similar passage. In addition, as was mentioned in the Introduction (page v), there are two longer biblical passages indicated, one chosen as appropriate to the liturgical season, the other enabling users to study a whole biblical book or part thereof.

At first sight, this is seems rather alarming. Do people really guide their lives, or believe that God is speaking through passages thus randomly chosen, even if they are chosen prayerfully? It is interesting to compare this with the way in which many people live their lives in the context of the no less randomly chosen items of news that feature in the press, radio, television and social media. What criteria guide the news editors whose task it is to decide what is newsworthy?

Newspaper editors have to please their owners and shareholders, and this means maximising the readership. One of the criteria for doing this is that bad news is more likely than good news to grab the attention of potential readers, unless there is good news about the sporting achievements of British teams and individual competitors. The concentration upon bad news means that the world of readers can be shaped by reports of natural disasters such as earthquakes, floods and famines in remote parts of the world, wars in countries that readers may be familiar with, political intrigues, scandals and corruption at home, and the never-ending obsession with the private lives of celebrities from royalty, television and films. One must, of course, be grateful for the freedom of the press and for investigative journalism, which brings to light scandals that might otherwise be covered up through the vested interests of the state, local authorities, multinational companies, and organisations such as the National Health Service. Nevertheless, it can be maintained that the world as presented in the press and similar media is a narrow interpretation of 'reality', dependent upon the interests and motivation of those choosing what will be presented. One has only to watch news programmes from countries other than Britain to see how the news and thus the presentation of 'reality' differ according to geography and culture.

Jochen Klepper did not live in a bubble that isolated him from the world around him so that he could concentrate on 'living in God's world as in Scripture', words which come from his diary entry for 22 January 1937.[101] True, there were times when he wanted to minimise his contacts with other people; but this was because the fame that the publication of *Der Vater* was bringing was tempting him to feel proud of his work,

---

[101] *Diary*, p. 417, 'Gotteswelt nach der Schrift'.

whereas his work was done in obedience to God, and in his awareness of being a sinner dependent upon God's grace.

Klepper was, in fact, fully aware of what was going on in the world in so far as it affected Germany and Europe, and made perceptive observations about the course of the Spanish Civil War, the involvement of the outside nations, and how this presaged becoming a full-scale European tragedy.[102] Of particular concern to Klepper was his exclusion from the State Literary Chamber and the consequence that he might be for ever banned from writing and publishing. He felt that his book *Das ewige Haus* was even more an obligation to God than *Der Vater* had been, so that all the efforts that were being made on his behalf to get the ban lifted, or to get him a special exemption, did not so much affect him personally as affect his divine mission as he understood it. The greatest success of *Der Vater* was that people were reading about kingship, Christ and the Old Testament in 1937![103]

It is necessary now to try to say in general how Klepper related to and used the *Losungen*, before following him through the year 1937 on the basis of his diary entries.

At the beginning of each day, Klepper seems to have copied down the *Losung*, either in the diary or in a notebook.[104] He did not confine his concern with the Bible simply to these passages, however. On 30 May 1937, for example, he notes in the diary, 'Have read Jeremiah 36 for the first time with awareness'.[105] That day was a Sunday and Jeremiah 36 may

---

[102] *Diary*, p. 456-7.
[103] *Diary*, p. 467, 'Am meisten staunen Hanni und ich in unserer Freude...dass dies alles von Königtum, Christus und das Alte Testament in einem Buche 1937 gesagt sein darf.'
[104] *Diary*, p. 445.
[105] *Diary*, p. 457 'Zum ersten Male Jeremiah 36 mit Bewusstsein gelesen'.

well have been one of the readings prescribed for Sunday worship, which were also printed in the *Losungen*. On 16 April 1937, he notes 'the whole of Psalm 38'.[106] However, in Klepper we are not dealing with a man who simply tried to be a Christian living in the world as shaped by the political circumstances of the day. The poet who wrote

> He wakes me every morning...
> He speaks as on the very day
> that he the world did make

believed that the reality in which his life was lived was God's reality and that that reality was mediated through the Bible, which was not an ancient text, but a means by which the living God spoke, guided, judged, pardoned and commissioned. Of course, Klepper worried about his everyday affairs and those of his wife and stepchildren. Of course, he sometimes wondered whether there would be enough income to support the family, especially when Jews (including his wife) were obliged to pay extra exorbitant taxes and levies on pretexts thought up by the National Socialist regime. But if it is possible to take seriously the words of Jesus, 'Take no anxious thought for the morrow... seek ye first the kingdom of God' (Matthew 6.25, 33), and in fact it is almost impossible for most Christians to do this, Klepper came close to doing so. It often left him in doubt and uncertainty, judged by standards that omitted any regard for God; but a certainty remained, and that certainty was underpinned by the daily encounter with the Bible and the belief that God's word was being spoken to him personally through it.

In chapter 5, I shall try to evaluate these beliefs and ask what, if anything, it can teach us about the nature and the use of the

---

[106] *Diary*, p. 443.

Bible. The rest of this chapter will go through Klepper's diary for 1937 to see how he interacted with the biblical passages that he noted down.

Klepper's baptism text was Isaiah 43.1: 'Fear not: for I have redeemed thee, I have called thee by thy name; thou art mine'. This text was bound to resonate with him as he went to Holy Communion on New Year's Day 1937 in the old church in Mariendorf, for it was the subject of Pastor Kurzreiter's address. On the following day, a Saturday, the New Testament version, 'Fear not, only believe', from Mark 5.36 was the *Losung* for the day. Three days later, on 5 January, the *Losung* from Isaiah 2.2 and 4 spoke of the Lord's house being established on the highest of all mountains, and Klepper was encouraged as he began his work on *Das ewige Haus*. The next day, the Feast of the Epiphany, when there was apparently no Protestant service, Klepper was glad that the *Losungen* marked the festival, even if his church did not.

Klepper had spent some of the days of the New Year break correcting the proofs of *Der Vater*, which he completed on 12 January. In his diary Klepper wrote:

> In the press, political relaxation. But under which aspects must we live and work? God must watch over one and be with his work, so that one is not overcome by paralysis and a deep tiredness. Otherwise it is not possible to live and work under the prayer, 'Thy kingdom come'.[107]

---

[107] *Diary*, p. 415 'In der Presse eine politische Entspannung. Aber unter welchen Aspecten müssen wir leben und wirken. Da muss Gott über einem wachen und mit einem an Werk sein, dass man nicht einer Lähmung und tiefer Müdigkeit verfällt. Anders kann man nicht mehr gelebt und gearbeitet sein als unter den "Dein Reich komme".'

On 22 January the *Losung* was from Isaiah 28.19: 'It shall be a vexation only to understand the report' [German, *Wort*]:

> The words from the Bible are to a frightening degree true, real and present. From such a word and the implications that arise from it, a day passes as when one has a serious illness.[108]

He went on to describe his situation as the necessity always to sin (*das Immer-Sündigen-Müssen*), and to dispute with God who had reconciled him. He noted that Paul and Luther had said everything on this subject; but one thing became ever clearer – the picture of God's world according to Scripture (*das Bild der Gotteswelt nach der Schrift*). Four days later, on 26 January, Klepper was reflecting on the attempts of Lene Haaske to reconcile him with his mother. Klepper praised this work, but implied that reconciliation had not touched his heart. He added, 'God is silent, just as he is silent about the book; but while silent he also acts'.[109]

For the remainder of January and the greater part of February, Klepper's greatest anxiety was how his book *Der Vater* would fare. Again, we must remember that his concern was for his mission as God's servant, and the hope of being able to continue this work, rather than his reputation as an author. On 22 February he noted that the propaganda minister, Goebbels, had boasted how the cultural life of the nation was being transformed by the elimination of all Jewish influence. He commented, 'There is no more hope; and faith means no

---

[108] *Diary*, p. 417, 'Die Bibelworte sind in einem furchtbaren Masse wahr und wirklich und gegenwärtig. Über solchem Worte und den Aspekten, die sich vor ihm auftun, geht ein Tag wie in schwerer Krankheit hin'.
[109] *Diary*, p. 418, 'Noch schweigt Gott, wie er auch zum Buche schweigt. Aber auch schweigend handelt er an uns'. God's silence about the book, presumably about whether it would be a success.

longer a human way but only God's purpose'.[110] The *Losung* for the day was Psalm 25.14: 'The secret of the Lord is with them that fear him'.

The secular news on 2 March was full of foreboding for Klepper and referred, among other things, to the full militarisation of Italy, and to Germany's demand for the restoration of the Colonies in South West Africa which had been lost after the 1914-18 war. 'It is a great blessing in this time', he wrote in the diary, 'to be "obsessed" by a plan of work that is not a *contra* but a *pro*, a *pro* the Cross.'[111] The advance copies of *Der Vater* arrived the next day. Because Klepper had been prevented from dedicating the book formally to his Jewish wife and stepdaughters, he presented them with copies personally inscribed.

On Saturday 13 March, Klepper was able to reflect that he had seen copies of *Der Vater* in bookshops, had been able to open a special bank account for the receipt of royalties, and to complete legal arrangements for his half-ownership of the house, something that would particularly ease inheritance tax problems for his Jewish stepdaughters. Typically, he wrote:

> All this must happen in the feeling and awareness of guilt. What applies to works is this: what God receives is his own generosity in our works; that is the picture in Job, also the righteousness of Christ for us. Luther.[112]

---

[110] *Diary*, p. 426, 'Hoffnung ist nicht mehr; und der Glaube meint ja nie einen menschlichen Weg, sondern immer nur das göttliche Ziel.'
[111] *Diary*, p. 429, 'Es ist eine grosse Gnade in dieser Zeit von einem Arbeitsplan "bessessen" sein zu dürfen, der kein *contra*, nur ein *pro* umschliesst: *pro cruce*.'
[112] *Diary*, p. 432, 'Dies alles muss geschehen im Gefühl und Bewusstsein der Schuld. Vom Werke gilt...was Gott annimmt, ist seine eigene Barmherzigkeit in unseren Werken, das ist die Gestalt Hiobs, bzw [beziehungsweise] die Gerechtigkeit Christi für uns. Luther.'

He was reminded of the *Losung* that stood at the head of the year 1937: 'It is a good thing that the heart be established with grace' (Hebrews 13.9).

The *Losung* for 22 March, Klepper's 34th birthday, was, as he noted, from Lamentations 3.37: 'Who is he that saith, and it cometh to pass, when the Lord commandeth it not?' Five days later, when the official notification of his dismissal from the State Literary Chamber arrived, the *Losung* was from Jeremiah 1.12: 'I will hasten [watch over] my word to perform it'. 'At such times', wrote Klepper, nothing counts or can happen except attention to the words of Scripture'.[113]

A long diary entry for 1 April is headed by the *Losung* from 2 Corinthians 1.13, 20, which ends, 'All God's promises are *Yes* in him and *Amen* in him to God's praise'. He notes that work on the new book has led him to look back over the entries in old note-books, in which he found the following entry, three days before completing the plan for *Der Vater*:

> One day faith seeks the ultimate from one, and one must hold God to his word: now, God of Israel, let your word be true. This is the most difficult thing for faith. Today: 'I speak it and also do it, says the Lord' (Ezekiel 37.14).[114]

That afternoon, in a meeting with Gustav Kilpper of the Deutsche Verlags-Anstalt, Klepper received approval for the project of *Das ewige Haus*. This lifted his spirits, as it meant that he could now spend his time as a full-time writer, funded by his publisher and the royalties. He felt that God had

---

[113] *Diary*, p. 434, 'In solchen Stunden kann nichts gelten und geschehen als der Blick auf die Worte der Schrift'.
[114] *Diary*, p. 437, 'Eines Tages verlangt fer Glaube das Äusserste von einem, und man muss Gott ein solches Wort hinhalten: Nun Gott Israels, lass deine Worte wahr werden. Das ist für den Glauben das Schwerste. Heute: Ich rede es und tue es auch, spricht der Herr, Hesek. 37.14.'

ameliorated the hardest blow, his exclusion from the State Literary Chamber, and one caused by his marriage. While others saw in this marriage a hindrance to Klepper's future as a writer, Klepper himself saw it from God's angle, as a rampart making a new life possible. 'Those whom God comforts, he comforts', noted Klepper, who was determined to see events only from that standpoint. The following day came the news that there needed to be a reprint of *Der Vater*, and Klepper was requested to correct the misprints of the first edition.

On 8 April Klepper posed the question, 'Before whom is one guilty?' and gave the answer, 'Always before God, who blesses in the conflict'. He noted that in Genesis 32.22-32 it was with God, not with Esau, that Jacob wrestled. Klepper summed up his approach to life thus:

> Not the tactical advance or retreat that each new day brings decides the attitude; what only matters is the divine word that is placed above each day.[115]

One of the strongest testimonies to Klepper's attachment to the *Losungen* came on 16 April. The *Losung* was from Hebrews 13.5: 'He has said, I will never leave thee nor forsake thee.' Klepper wrote,

> Without such words one could hardly survive. In the morning one writes them down and in the evening they have been explained by what has happened.[116]

---

[115] *Diary*, p. 441, 'Nicht die taktische Fortschritt oder Rückschritt, den ein neuer Tag bringt, entscheidet die Haltung, sondern das allein ist wichtig, welches Wort über den Tag gestellt ist.'

[116] *Diary*, p. 442, 'Ohne solche Worten wäre es kaum zu ertragen. Am Morgen schreibt man sie nieder und am Abend sind sie durch die Ereignisse ausgelegt.'

Six days later he was extending this belief:

> The Bible verse that I wrote down this morning has meant even more than the day has brought as interpretation.

The verse in question was Job 42.2: 'I know that thou canst do everything and that no thought can be withholden from thee'. Klepper continued;

> No created mortal should speak thus to his Creator, except in Christ. Nothing is too hard for him, except that our sins have caused him great trouble.[117]

As the representations for Klepper's reinstatement in the Literary Chamber went on behind the scenes, Klepper was reassured on 4 June by two biblical passages. The first was the *Losung*, 'It is a precious thing that the heart remains firm'. The second was from Revelation 3.8, 'Behold, I have set before thee an open door, and no man can shut it: for thou hast a little strength, and hast kept my word, and hast not denied my name'. From this Klepper drew the following conclusion:

> No book that God wills to be written, the God who so often says to someone in Scripture: Write! will remain unwritten, notwithstanding the worthiness or unworthiness of the writer or how he is affected by other people. Only so can I think of my bitter situation.[118]

There is a long diary entry for Sunday 6 June that incidentally sheds light on how Klepper saw his work as a Christian writer. It sets out from the *Losung* from Hebrews 12.7: 'If ye endure chastening, God dealeth with you as a son; for what

---

[117] *Diary*, p. 445, 'Kein Geschöpf, das nicht so zu seinem Schöpfer eimal – nun aber in Christo! – sprechen müsste! Nicht ist ihm zu schwer, aber mit unserer Sünde haben wir ihm Mühe gemacht.'

[118] *Diary*, p. 460-1, 'Kein Buch, dass Gott geschrieben haben will – der so oft in der Schrift zu einem sprach Schreibe! – wird, über Wert und Unwert der Person des Schreibenden hinweg, und wenn auch behaftet mit allen Menschen, ungeschrieben werden. So, nur so darf ich meine bittere Lage betrachten.'

son is he who whom the father chasteneth not?' This leads to a long and thoughtful reflection upon what Klepper calls 'gracious corrections' (*gnädige Zurechtweisungen*). He argues that while people deserve the set-backs and problems they encounter, these can also be seen as the hidden work of God, whose undeserved grace more than suffices for those who can recognise this and render thanks to God. Klepper sums up his God-given task as he sees it, the task of dependence upon God's justificatory grace alongside all human failings, as follows:

> Biblical interpretation through narrative.
>
> Narrative whose subject is the things that make up life: order, security.
>
> Biblical interpretation and definition of terms told from the standpoint of a life guided by God.[119]

There then follows a remarkable passage, in which Klepper sees the Christian life in terms of a symphony which contains both polyphony and dissonance, and throughout which runs the thread of a chorale which continues when the symphony ends. Klepper cites the following words:

> That suffering I should praise him
> is that which he desires.

The following week he was informed by the president of the Literary Chamber that his suspension had been temporarily postponed and that in the meantime he could continue his writing.[120]

---

[119] *Diary*, pp. 462-3, 'Schriftauslegung durch Erzählung. Erzählung, die zum Gegenstand hat Elemente, welche das Leben bestimmen; etwas 'Ordnung' 'Sicherheit' ... Die Schriftauslegung und Begriffsbestimmung erzählt als von Gott geführtes Leben.'
[120] *Diary*, pp. 463-4.

In August 1937 Klepper was thus able to plunge ever more deeply into his work on *Das ewige Haus*, and although it was centred upon Luther's wife, Katharina, he found that he could only do his work by seeing her in the light of Luther. Nevertheless, he and Hanni spent the beginning of September visiting places that were in different ways associated with Katharina and her flight from the convent of Marienthron, near Grimma, to the south-east of Leipzig. An interesting observation made in the diary for 16 August is that the history of the house (that is, Luther's domestic house) is also the history of the origin of the German Bible. Precisely what Klepper meant by this is not clear. The admittedly sketchy plan of *Das ewige Haus* does not mention it, and neither is there any connection made between Luther's translation and his domestic circumstances in standard works such as Bornkamm's *Luther in Mid-Career*.[121] Perhaps Klepper meant that the domestic care that Katharina provided, especially during Luther's illnesses, enabled translation work to be done that would otherwise have been impossible.

Whenever Klepper came across a *Losung* that mentioned a house, he took this as a reference to his current work. The *Losung* for 26 August was from Hebrews 3.6: 'Christ as a son over his own house; whose house we are, if we hold fast the confidence and the rejoicing of the hope firm unto the end'. He commented, 'Such words soothe (*beschwichtigen*) the heart in thoughts on the title of the new book'.[122]

On Sunday 29 August he wrote,

> I must think a great deal about the Gospel for this Sunday (it was the 14th after Trinity and the Gospel was Luke

---

[121] H. Bornkamm, *Luther in Mid-Career 1521-1530*, London: Darton, Longman and Todd, 1983.
[122] *Diary*, p. 482.

17.11-19) about the ten lepers which the Sunday service so ignored. When lepers presented themselves in the temple as already clean on the command of Christ and his redeeming authority, that is the possibility of being clean. John 15.3. This Gospel is one of the most helpful for me!

This may well have been the inspiration for the poem that he composed on John 15.3 (see p. 91).[123]

On 5 October the *Losung* was Psalm 81.7: 'Thou calledst in trouble, and I delivered thee; I answered thee in the secret place of thunder.' Klepper commented:

> Always, when the heart is bitter and tired, always, when the task is too great, comes the simple *Losung*: there is no loss that 'occurs without the Lord's command'. There is no gift for which he may not be thanked. There is no guilt that is not forgiven by him to save the one that is his secret and which I need not experience. There is no suffering and endeavour that cannot be transformed and valued by him to my salvation and his honour, because everything comes before him in Christ's name.[124]

On 11 October the *Losung* was Genesis 15.8: 'And he said, Lord GOD, whereby shall I know that I shall inherit it?' Klepper obviously felt himself to be under unbearable pressures in his attempt to get on with his work for *Das ewige Haus*. He had resolved on 9 October to withdraw as much as

---

[123] *Diary*, p. 487, 'Ich muss heut viel an das Evangelium dieses Sonntags von den zehn Aussätzigen denken, vor dem der Gottesdienst so versagte. Als Aussätziger sich schon als rein im Tempel zeigen auf Christi Geheiß und aus seiner erlösendern Vollmacht: das ist die Mögichkeit, rein zu sein. Johannes 15.3! Dieses Evangelium wird mir zu einem der hilfreichsten.'

[124] *Diary*, p. 508, 'Immer wieder wenn das Herz bitter und müde ist, immer wieder wenn der Anspruch sich vermisste, kommt die einfache Losung: Es ist kein Verlust, der "ohne des Herrn Befehl geschieht", ist keine Gabe, für die ihm nicht gedankt werden darf. Es gibt – ausser dieser einen, die sein Geheimnis bleibt und die ich nicht zu erfahren brauche – keine Schuld, die nicht durch ihn vergeben ist. Es gibt kein Leiden und Tun, das nicht, weil alles in Christi Namen vor ihm gebracht wird, von ihm gewendet und gewertet kann zu meinem Heil und seiner Ehre.'

possible from human contact. On 11 October he commented on the wall that must be erected between him and the world:

> It doesn't come from me, it is not anger, or bitterness, or despair, or retreat, or ingratitude, or asceticism; it is the demand of the work and also from God! It will be finished through the pain and weariness of the heart and spirit.[125]

The last phrase of the *Losung* for 11 December was the famous passage from Habakkuk 2.4 that was so important for Paul: 'The righteous shall live by faith'. 'Shall live by faith', wrote Klepper, 'this is the final, single, greatest and most valuable possibility, and it includes everything'.[126] This, perhaps, is a fitting place to end this chapter.

---

[125] *Diary*, p. 512, 'Die ist nicht von mir, nicht Zorn, Verbitterung, Enttäuschung, Abkehr oder auch Undank, nicht Askese: die ist Mühsal der Arbeit und also von Gott! Unter Schmerz und Müdigkeit des Herzens und Geistes wird sie errichtet.'

[126] *Diary*, p. 527, 'Seines Glaubens leben: dies ist die letzte, einzige, grösste noch gewährte Möglichkeit: und sie umschliesst alles.'

CHAPTER 5

'Living in God's World, as in Scripture'
A Critical Appreciation

Klepper's attempts to live his life in the light of the *Losungen* seem to me to raise two main questions, which will be treated in two sections. The first question consists of the two closely related issues: what view of the Bible, and what view of what it means to be human, are implied in Klepper's attempt? The second main question is whether it is credible for readings designed to be used by large number of readers to be applicable to the highly personal situations of individual users.

I

That there is no current agreement in the churches or among scholars about the correct way to understand and use the Bible goes without saying; and in the past fifty years, in academic circles, the Bible has been read and used from many different perspectives, including feminist, womanist, colonialist, liberation and ecological standpoints. This modern emphasis on diversity contrasts with earlier periods in the Church's history, where the Bible was not allowed to speak with its own voice, but was regarded as a depository of proof texts to support doctrines that had been worked out by the various churches. Even so, in these earlier periods there was much creative and personal use of the Bible as God's Word, for private meditation or public preaching.

The Reformation of the sixteenth century brought great changes in the study and use of the Bible; but in many Protestant circles there developed a kind of fundamentalism that saw the Bible as a divinely-written authority on all matters of history, astronomy and science. Although this view was challenged by notable Christian leaders, such as John Calvin and Richard Baxter, it persists today in those churches that reject Darwinian theories of evolution on the grounds that they contradict the teaching of Genesis chapter 1 on how the universe came into being. The suggestion that the Bible should be studied 'like any other book' was strongly resisted in Britain in the nineteenth century, as was the steady and inevitable encroachment of biblical criticism in the nineteenth and twentieth centuries; and it is still the case that in many Protestant churches of Africa and Central and Southern America, not to mention parts of the United States, a literalist fundamentalist outlook dominates the way in which the Bible is regarded and used.

Klepper was not a fundamentalist. He had studied under Ernst Lohmeyer in Breslau, among others. He was, however, a convinced Lutheran, whose Christian faith centred upon the twin axes of human sinfulness and the miracle of divine mercy mediated through Jesus Christ. This faith gave a 'centre' to the way that he understood the Bible. Is this a viable way of using the Bible today?

This raises the related matter of how the question, 'What does it mean to be human?' is to be answered, and whether it is to be answered in a secular or a theological way. Those who approach the Bible from liberation, feminist, womanist and ecological perspectives are usually, but not necessarily, motivated by secular, humanist standpoints in relation to what it means to be human; and it must be emphasized that there is nothing wrong with this. If the Bible resonates with, and gives support to, secular humanistic longings for economic, ecological and gender justice in today's world, who can object? Some of the greatest prophetic visions of a new and just order are to be found in the Old Testament. The relevant question that this chapter is asking, however, is not whether a method of using the Bible can be found that 'trumps' all other methods, but whether Klepper's approach, with its theological understanding of what it means to be human, is viable in today's world, and intellectually sustainable.

Klepper's view of what it means to be human was Pauline and Lutheran. Humanity is sinful and in need of God's forgiving grace, which is received by faith which God inspires through Jesus Christ. The forgiven sinner remains a sinner until death, dependent always until that moment upon the continuing grace of God. This was Klepper's own experience and conviction, and one that he applied to his portrayal of Frederick William. How can a sinful man be a ruler?

At first sight, this Reformation Pauline view of what it means to be human does not seem to offer much help for understanding the Bible, especially the Old Testament, which forms most of the Bible. Deeper reflection indicates, however, that this view can be found throughout the Old Testament. One of the remarkable features of the Old Testament is the way in which it presents the chief representatives of the faith of Israel as deeply flawed personalities, and the people as a whole as constantly failing to appreciate God's mercy or to meet his demands. I should make it clear that I understand the personalities that I shall discuss here not as historical figures but, more importantly, as the product of the cultural memory of the prophetic and priestly circles in which the traditions about the personalities were transmitted and shaped. They are 'ideal types' who express and encapsulate the ambiguities of what happens when people encounter and seek to follow the God of the Bible.

Abraham is an important person with whom to begin, because he features so prominently in Paul's use of the Old Testament as the person whose faith enables God to by-pass the law, so to speak (see Romans 4.1-25, Galatians 3.6-18). That Abraham is a flawed character is shown by his attempts to get an heir by adoption (Genesis 15.2) and surrogacy (Genesis 16.1-6), when God has promised that he would have offspring. His casting out of Ishmael and Hagar (Genesis 21.9-21) is hardly to his credit, neither is his denial that Sarah is his wife when he feels his life to be threatened by Pharaoh (Genesis 12.10-20) and Abimelech (Genesis 20.1-18). Alongside these narratives, of course, must be set Abraham's willingness to offer Isaac in sacrifice (Genesis 22). No one is completely flawed. God's grace can bring changes to those who accept it.

Jacob, the ancestor of the twelve tribes, is a trickster who defrauds his brother Esau of his birthright (Genesis 25.29-34), and his father's blessing (Genesis 27.1-40), and his uncle Laban of his sheep and cattle and household gods (Genesis 30.30-43 and 31.1-55), while his prayer to God at Bethel (Genesis 28.20-22) seems to make Jacob's acknowledgement of God dependent upon God fulfilling Jacob's wishes. His prayer before he mysteriously wrestles with God (Genesis 32.9-11) shows how God's grace has softened the selfish trickster, and brings a gracious response from God: 'I will surely do thee good, and make thy seed as the sand of the sea, which cannot be numbered for multitude (Genesis 32.12).

The portrait of Moses is that of a tragic figure, rejected by the people he had led out of slavery and finally denied entrance to the Promised Land. Perhaps it is to David that we should turn next, because not only is he the 'man after God's own heart' (1 Samuel 13.14), who cynically commits adultery with the wife of one of his soldiers and then arranges for that soldier to be killed in battle (2 Samuel 11), but because he is traditionally held to be the author of the Psalms, or many of them. Of course, modern scholarship does not accept that claim, nor does it accept as historically true the many psalm titles that locate particular psalms in the life of David, a notable example being the title that links Psalm 51 with David's penitence in the affair of Bathsheba. But we are dealing here with the cultural memory of the priestly and prophetic traditions, and in this regard, the linking of the authorship of the Psalms to David is significant. It means that readers are meant to see Israel's greatest king, the man after God's own heart, and the figure from whom hopes for a future coming ruler spring, as a humble man, assailed by doubts, needing forgiveness and yet able to offer God his praise and worship. The David that the Psalms imply is very close to Klepper's sinner sustained by God's mercy and love.

So far, I have dealt with individual figures in the Old Testament, as presented by the cultural memory of the circles that gave the Old Testament its final form. I could enlarge that account by discussing the tragic figure of Jeremiah, who accuses God of deceiving him (Jeremiah 27), or by considering Job, who has many harsh things to say about God, yet who is finally vindicated. However, I want to move to the latter chapters of Isaiah, 40-66. These chapters were very precious to Klepper. His baptism text, 'Fear not: for I have redeemed thee, I have called thee by thy name; thou art mine' (Isaiah 43.1), came from these chapters, and they seem to have figured frequently in the *Losungen* on which he commented.

The important thing about these chapters is that the people of God, viewed corporately, is addressed, usually by the name of Jacob, and appears as a group oppressed by guilt and uncertainty, yet assured time and again of God's mercy and forgiveness and hope for the future. No doubt the historical background to these chapters, whether they were composed in Babylon or Palestine, is the destruction of the Jerusalem temple in 587 BC, and the belief that this catastrophe had been brought upon the people by their unfaithfulness to God and that of their forefathers. The important thing is that the people addressed in these chapters is a people that are only too aware of past failures and present hopelessness, and it is no accident that Isaiah 40 begins with a command to the prophet to comfort his people. Klepper's baptism text was similarly a word of reassurance, spoken in that situation. There is, of course, far more of the Old Testament than I have briefly touched upon here, and I would not want to claim that what I am arguing could satisfactorily explain the Book of Proverbs, for example. However, I hope that I have said enough to be able to make the claim that, whatever else the Old Testament is about, significant parts of it can be understood in terms of a humanity, whether individually or corporate, that is seen to be fragile and flawed and yet the recipient of the mercy and forgiveness of God, whose mercy and forbearance are able to outlast the failures and backslidings of the people.

The next move is to argue that the reason why 'what it means to be human' in the Bible can be answered in terms of a humanity flawed and fragile, yet the undeserved recipient of God's mercy and forgiveness, is because one of the main purposes of the Bible is to enable readers to experience for themselves the mercy and forgiveness of God about which the Bible speaks. Traditionally, the Bible has been seen as 'revelation', in the sense of conveying information about God and the world; and it is this view of revelation as information that is behind attempts to pit the description of the creation of the world in Genesis 1 against the findings of modern science. It would be wrong to deny that the Bible contains information. It remains a primary source of information about the history of Ancient Israel, the life and teaching of Jesus, and the beginnings of Christianity; but there is more to it than that.

One of the great discoveries of Martin Luther, and we remember that Jochen Klepper was an ardent Lutheran, was that the qualities attributed to God in the Bible do not describe what God *is* but what he *does*, and that this fact enables readers and hearers of the Bible to be brought into contact with those things that God does, in a personal way. Luther discovered that the phrase, 'the righteousness of God', means God working to put people right with himself; and that realisation brought about a complete change in Luther's life, because it brought him into a relationship with God in which, while he remained a sinner in need of God's grace, he had the reassurance that that grace was always available. In turn, this discovery gave birth to faith, faith being the divine gift by which God's mercy and grace were received. Luther went on to define other divine attributes of God in a similar way: God's wisdom is that which makes people wise, his might is that which empowers people, and so on.

The Old Testament is replete with passages which speak of God in such a way as to do two things: to assert that it is God's purpose to be in relationship with human beings, that is, to love them, and secondly, to be the means by which that relationship is established and maintained. Deuteronomy 7.7-8 says to God's people, Israel:

> The LORD did not set his love upon you, nor choose you, because ye were more in number than any people; for ye were the fewest of all people: but because the LORD loved you, and because he would keep the oath which he has sworn unto your fathers, hath the LORD brought you out with a mighty hand, and redeemed you out of the house of bondmen, from the hand of Pharaoh king of Egypt.

It goes on to describe the relationship of God with his people on the analogy of a parent whose proper task it is, in love, to punish and correct a child as it grows up. A passage in Deuteronomy 9 about the possession of the land of Canaan declares,

> Understand therefore, that the LORD thy God giveth thee not this good land to possess it for thy righteousness; for thou art a stiffnecked people. Remember, and forget not, how that thou provokedst the LORD thy God to wrath in the wilderness: from the day that thou didst depart out of the land of Egypt, until ye came unto this place, ye have been rebellious against the LORD. (Deuteronomy 9.6-7)

This reference to the traditions of the wilderness wanderings in the books of Exodus and Numbers is a reminder of the importance of these foundation narratives in the Old Testament. Here is a people, newly freed from slavery, sustained by God's presence in the pillar of cloud by day and the pillar of fire by night, and by the Tent of Meeting, yet constantly dissatisfied with their lot. These narratives vividly portray the redeemed but sinful people who are totally dependent in the wilderness upon God's provision. Indeed, the importance of the wilderness is precisely that, of itself, it is not able to sustain the people without God.

The theme of God's struggles, so to speak, with his redeemed people can be traced through the so-called historical books to the trauma of Jerusalem's destruction and the people's return from captivity. It is also a theme found in the prophets, especially Hosea, where the famous words occur,

> When Israel was a child then I loved him, and called my son out of Egypt (Hosea 11.1).

The passage goes on to speak of how the people were unfaithful, culminating in the words

> How shall I give thee up, Ephraim? How shall I deliver thee, Israel...I will not execute the fierceness of mine anger. I will not return to destroy Ephraim: for I am God, and not a man; the Holy One in the midst of thee (Hosea 11. 8-9).

A similar theme is explored in Ezekiel 16, where the people is likened to a baby girl abandoned at birth, whom God rescues and adopts, but who goes after lovers to whom she owes nothing, except their desire to exploit her.

The Old Testament points beyond itself to hopes for a future in which a solution will be found to the problem that a redeemed people, loved and sustained by God, is unable or unwilling to be loved and sustained. Jeremiah 31.31 speaks of a new covenant, unlike the one made at the time of the Exodus from Egypt. Ezekiel 36.26-7 speaks of God creating a new heart in the people and of putting his spirit within them.

In the New Testament, God's word made flesh in Jesus seeks the ungodly and affirms and transforms them. His death and resurrection become the redeeming events, which break the power of sin and evil under whose sway men and women live, the proclamation of which, while folly to Greeks and a stumbling block to Jews, is the power of God for salvation (1 Corinthians 1.18). It is a proclamation which awakens faith, which is the discovery of the undeserved forgiveness and mercy of God, and the means and the dimension by which the power of sin is broken and believers live in the presence of God.

Going back to the Old Testament, the very existence of the prophets is testimony to the function of what is proclaimed to enable hearers to turn and relate to God. The primary task of the prophets is not to impart information. Their message is 'repent; 'seek me'; and in Isaiah 55.11 God declares that his word will not return to him void,

> but it shall accomplish that which I please, and it shall prosper in the thing whereto I sent it.

The answer to the first question posed at the beginning of this section can be summed up as follows. The Bible bears witness to an interaction between God and his people and individuals within his people, in which God's mercy is made manifest to frail, fragile and transient humanity. This interaction is manifested supremely in Jesus Christ. In turn, the Bible is the means by which hearers and readers may themselves be confronted by God's condemning and reconciling word, and know themselves to be, in Luther's language, at one and the same time sinners and justified by God's grace. Such a view accords fully with Klepper's understanding and use of the Bible.

II

Is it credible for *Losungen*, designed to be used by a large number of people, to be applicable to the highly personal situations of individual users?

The answer to this question is clearly 'no' if people use the *Losungen* to predict their future or to understand details of their present situations. Such a view makes the Bible subservient to their needs, so that it then differs little from the horoscopes that people consult in newspapers and magazines. A good place to begin in considering this question is to ask Klepper's question as applied to Frederick William: how can a Christian, that is, someone aware of being at the same time a sinner and justified by God's grace, be a ruler? The question can be extended. How can a Christian, someone aware of being at one and the same time a sinner and justified by God's grace, be a writer, or a scholar, or a medical doctor, or an airline pilot, or a shop worker, or whatever other role one cares to add? The answer will be different for each individual, but the awareness of being a justified sinner will surely make, or should make, a profound difference to how these roles and functions are perceived and lived out. The function of the readings will be to inspire and reassure users of God's presence in their lives, and of their continual need of his undeserved mercy. The *Losungen* will not change the world as interpreted and presented by the profit-driven purveyors of local and national news. They will enable the readers of the *Losungen* to put that perceived world into the context of God's reality, as conveyed by the Bible and their own local and domestic tasks in the world as Christians.

This, I believe, is how Klepper saw things. He believed that God had called him to be a writer and poet, and that this calling was not intended to bring him fame or wealth, but intended to enable him to convey to others Klepper's conviction that God is a God who speaks, and whose undeserved grace and mercy sustain those who know their need of it. There is more to it than that, of course. The Bible is not there simply to reassure people of God's presence in their daily lives; it contains visions of a world transformed by the victory over evil of God's non-coercive love. It speaks of eternity, and eternal life, of all things taking their origin from and being summed up in Jesus Christ. These things must also be taken into account when negotiating the demands of everyday life in the particularities of individuals.

For Klepper, the Christian liturgical year, with its special seasons, played an important part in the way his life was framed. He also had a deep conviction that God's word, as said in Isaiah 55.11, would prosper in the thing whereto it was sent. In one way, this proved to be mistaken. *Das ewige Haus*, which Klepper believed to be his greatest God-given task, was never completed. It was frustrated by the evil of a regime that glorified a view of part of humanity as that of a super race with the right and duty to oppress and exterminate 'inferior' specimens. Yet it was not this regime that endured; and the fact that Klepper's writings continue to inspire and amaze is itself testimony the belief that God's word endures for ever, and that Jochen Klepper is a remarkable witness to that belief. His vision of being able to live in God's world as determined by scripture is not an empty hope, but one that has the power to direct and transform Christian living today.

Bibliography

Baum, M.
Jochen Klepper, Schwarzenfeld: Neufeld Verlag, 2011

Bayreuth, Wilhelmine von
Memoiren, Leipzig: Insel-Verlag, 1923

Bornkamm, H.
Luther in Mid-Career 1521-1530, London: Darton, Longman and Todd, 1983

Feuerstein-Prasser, K.
Die preußischen Königinnen, Munich: Piper Verlag, 2008

Ihlenfeld, K.
Freundschaft mit Jochen Klepper, Windeck: Windecker Verlag, 1979

Jonas, I.
Jochen Klepper. Dichter und Zeuge. Ein Lebensbild, Berlin: Christlicher Zeitschriftenverlag, no date

Klepper, J.
Der Kahn der fröhlichen Leute (1933), Fischer: Frankfurt, 1955

Klepper, J.
Der Vater. Roman eines Königs (1937), Munich: Deutsche Taschenbuch Verlag, 2003

Klepper, J.
In tormentis pinxit. Briefe und Bilder des Soldatenkönigs, Stuttgart: Deutsche Verlags-Anstalt, 1938.

Klepper, J.
Der König und die Stillen im Lande, Witten/Berlin: Eckart Verlag, 1938.

Klepper, J.
Kyrie. Geistliche Lieder [1938], Bielefeld: Luther-Verlag, 1950

Klepper, J.
Unter dem Schatten deiner Flügel. Aus den Tagebüchern der Jahre 1932-1942. Mit einem Geleitwort von Reinhold Schneider, Stuttgart: Deutsche Verlags-Anstalt, 1955

Klepper, J.
Die Flucht der Katharina von Bora, Aus dem Nachlaß herausgegeben und eingeleitet von Karl Pagel, Berlin: Evangelische Verlagsanstalt, 1956 [Stuttgart: Deutsche Verlags-Anstalt, 1951]

Klepper, J.
Überwindung. Tagebücher und Aufzeichnungen aus dem Kriege, Stuttgart: Deutsche Verlags-Anstalt, 1958

Klepper, J.
Gast und Fremdling. Briefe an Freunde (ed. Eva-Juliane Meschke), Witten and Berlin: Eckart Verlag, 1960

Klepper, J.
Nachspiel. Aufsätze des Erzählers, Witten and Berlin: Eckart-Verlag, 1960

Klepper, J.
Ziel der Zeit. Die gesammelten Gedichte, Bielefeld: Luther Verlag, 1980

Mann, O. (ed.)
Christliche Dichter im 20. Jahrhundert. Beiträge zur Europäischen Literatur, Bern and Munich: Francke Verlag, 1968

Mascher, B.
'Jochen Klepper' in O. Mann (ed.), *Christliche Dichter im 20. Jahrhundert. Beiträge zur Europäischen Literatur*, Bern and Munich: Francke Verlag, 1968, pp. 398-409

Otto, W.
'Ernst Lohmeyer und Jochen Klepper' in W. Otto (ed.), *Freiheit in der Gebundenheit. Zur Erinnerung an den Theologen Ernst Lohmeyer anläßlich seines 100. Geburtstages*, Göttingen: Vandenhoeck & Ruprecht, 1990, pp. 135-180

Reske, H.
In seinem Wort mein Glück. Jochem Kleppers Ringen mit der Bibel in seinen Tagebüchern, Neukirchen-Vluyn: Aussat Verlag, 2008

Riemschneider, E. G. (ed.)
Jochen Klepper. Briefwechsel 1925-1942, Stuttgart: Deutsche Verlags-Anstalt, 1973

Schneider, R.
Die Hohenzollern. Tragik und Königtum, Leipzig: Verlag Jakob Hegner, 1933

Thalmann, R.
Jochen Klepper. Ein Leben zwischen Idyllen und Katastrophen, Munich: Kaiser Verlag, 1977

Wallmann, J.
'Ein Vermächtnis Kaiser Wilhelm II. Was hat Walter Grundmanns Eisenacher "Entjudungsinstitut" mit Martin Luther zu tun?' in *Zeitschrift für Theologie und Kirche* 114 (2017), pp. 289-314

Wentorf, R.
Jochen Klepper. Ein Dichter im Dennoch, Giessen and Basel: Brunnen-Verlag, 1967

Biblical References

OLD TESTAMENT		
Genesis		
1	110, 113	
1.2	86	
12.10-20	110	
15.2	110	
15.8	105	
16.1-6	110	
20.1-18	110	
21.9-21	110	
22	110	
25.29-34	110	
27.1-40	110	
28.20-22	111	
30.30-43	110	
31.1-55	111	
32.9-11, 12	111	
32.22-32	101	
Exodus	114	
Numbers	114	
Deuteronomy		
7.7-8	114	
9.6-7	114	
1 Samuel		
13.14	111	
2 Samuel		
11	111	
Job	99, 112	
42.2	102	
Psalms	111	
25.14	99	
27.4-5	66	
35.20	27	
38	96	
51	111	
81.7	105	
130	42	

Proverbs	112	
20.28	90	
Isaiah		
2.2, 4	97	
28.19	98	
33.17-18	26	
37.31	29	
40-66	112	
43.1	97, 112	
48.1-11	50-1	
50	86-7	
50.4	84	
50.4-5, 8	85	
55.11	116, 118	
Jeremiah		
1.12	100	
15.16	89	
23.28	25	
27	112	
31.31	115	
36	95	
Lamentations		
3.37	100	
Ezekiel		
16	115	
36.26-7	115	
37.14	100	
Hosea		
11.1, 8-9	115	
Habakkuk		
2.4	106	
NEW TESTAMENT		
Matthew		
6.25, 33	96	
7.1	41	
Mark		
5.36	97	

Luke		
17.11-19	104-105	
John		
15.3	91, 105	
Romans		
4.1-25	110	
8.37-39	41	
1 Corinthians		
1.18	116	
6.19-20	41	
10.13	76	
13.12	81	
2 Corinthians		
1.13, 20	100	
4.6	86	
Galatians		
3.6-18	110	
Ephesians		
6.10-17	41	
Philippians		
2.8	88	
5.2-9	87	
Hebrews		
1.1-3	87	
3.6	104	
11.10	68	
11.17, 19	75	
12.7	102	
13.5	101	
13.9	100	
1 Peter		
3.8-17	32	
1 John		
3.2	87	
Revelation		
3.8	102	

Index

Page numbers in bold refer to major entries on a topic

Abraham, 75, 110
Anti-Semitism, 16, 17, 19, 24
   see also Jewish persecution
Baum, M., 119
Bäumer, G., 43
Baxter, R., 108
Bayreuth, W. von, 76, 78
Beheim-Schwarzbach, M., 43
Bergengruen, W., 43
Berlin, 19, 20, 21, 24-5, 28, 35-6, 37, 39, 60-2, 80
Berliner Funk (Berlin Radio), 20-1
Beuthen an der Oder (Bytom Odrzański), 12, 15, 17, 45
Bible, use of, 96-7, 107-109, 116
Bora, Katharina von –
   14, 29-30, 44, 65, 104
   see also Klepper, J.: Novels – *Das ewige Haus* and *The Flight of Katharina von Bora*
Bornkamm, H., 104
Braun, H., 20-1
Breslau, 15, 16, 19, 24
Breslau, University of –
   13, 15, 29, 108
Calvin, J., 108
Confessing Church, the, 31-2, 33
Croydon, 31
David (king), 111
Deutsche Verlags-Anstalt, 20, 100
Die Losungen, 12, **93-106, 107-118**

Dietrich Reimer Verlag, 38-9
Dresden, 69, 70-1
Eckart Verlag, 28, 43, 86
Eichmann, Adolf, 41
Erlangen, University of, 13
Evangelisches Gesangbuch, 86
Feuerstein-Prasser, K., 119
'Forwards' (Social Democratic journal), 16
Francke, A. H., 14, 15-16, 28
Frederick II of Prussia, 33, 54, 71, 72, 73-7,
Frederick William I of Prussia –
   Klepper's books on, 11, 14, 16, 17, 21-2, 27-8, 30, 33, 36, 37, 81-3, 117
   portrayed in *Der Vater*, **51-83**
   see also Ragotin
Freylinghausen, J. A., 28, 70
Frick, W., 37, 40-1
Friederike Luise of Prussia, Princess, 71-2, 76, 78
Fromm, E., 12
Fundamentalism, Christian, 108
George I of England, 66, 67
George II of England, 67, 72
George, S., 14
Glogau (Głogów), 12, 13, 18
Goebbels, J., 37, 98
Göring, H., 27
Gottschalk, J., 37-8

Gundolf, F., 14
Haaske, L., 98
Hacker, B., 12
Halle, 28, 70, 75, 78
Hermann, R., 13, 15, 16 n.8, 29, 34
Herrnhuter *Losungen*
   see *Die Losungen*
Herrnhuter Moravians
   see Moravian Brotherhood
Hindenburg, P. von, 68
Hitler, A., 12, 17, 21, 22, 28, 33, 38, 43, 68, 70
Hohenzollern family, 21
Ihlenfeld, K., 43, 49
Jacob, 101, 110-111, 112
Jeremiah (as prophet), 112
Jewish persecution –
   compulsory divorce of non-Aryan spouses, 37, 38, 41
   deportation of, 32, 37-8, 39
   elimination of Jewish culture, 82, 98, 118
   factory work, 36
   'privileged' marriages, 40
   restrictions on, 36, 38
   taxes and levies, 96
   yellow star, 36
Jonas, I., 120
Kaiser William II (exiled), 26, 82,
Kilpper, G., 100
Klepper, Georg, 12, 16-17
Klepper, Jochen: Biography -
   generally, **11-42**
   baptism text, 97, 112
   Berlin, house in, 19, 20, 24, 28
   birth, 12
   Breslau, lodgings in, 16, 24
   Breslau, University of, 13, 15, 29, 108
   career change, 13, 14, 29
   Christian writing, his dedication to, 29
   death, 11, 16, 37-8, 40-2
   elegance, his love of, 13, 17
   Erlangen, University of, 13
   finances, 17, 20, 21, 96, 99, 100
   funeral, 41-2
   health, his, 14
   insomnia, 34, 88
   marriage, 17-18, 34, 40, 45, 101
   military service, 33, 34-7, 88
   Nikolassee, his church in, 28, 32, 33, 41
   Nikolassee, his house in, 28, 31, 41
   Oder region, influence of, 12, 49
   parents, 12, 16-17, 36
   school, 12-13
   sculpture of 'Christ blessing', 40, 41
   State Literary Chamber, his suspension from, 26, 95, 100, 101, 102, 103
   Silesian idioms, his use of, 49
   Social Democratic Party, his membership of, 19
   stability, his need for, 29
   work for –
      Berlin Radio, 20-1
      Deutsche Verlags-Anstalt, 20, 100
      Dietrich Reimer Verlag, 38-9

Protestant Press Agency, 15, 20, 30
Silesian Broadcasting Company, 15
writing, restrictions on, 26-7
Würzburg, holiday, 39-40

Klepper, Jochen: Family –
father –
   see Klepper, Georg
mother, 12-13, 16, 36, 98
stepdaughters –
   see Stein, Brigitte
   see Stein, Renate
wife – see Klepper, Johanna

Klepper, Jochen: Diaries –
generally, 11-12, 34
compulsive diarist, 11
Die Losungen, his diary comments on, 12, **95-106**
Overcoming, 11, 33, 34
Under the shadow of thy wings, 11

Klepper, Jochen: Journalism –
'Die Zeitwende', 43
'Forwards', 16
'Our Church', 15
Protestant Press Agency, his work for, 15, 20, 30
radio broadcasting, 15, 20-1

Klepper, Jochen: Novels –
generally, 11-13, 17-23
Christian novelist, his views on nature of, **44-83**
parallels with his life, 46
proposed filming of, 17, 18, 22-3, 30, 37

The Barge of Joyful People (Der Kahn der fröhlichen Leute), 19-21, 23, 43, 44, **45-49**
The Eternal House (Das ewige Haus), 29-30, 38, 83, 95, 97, 100, 104, 105, 118
The Father (Der Vater), 12, 21-3, 26, 36, 44, **51-83**, 94-5, 97, 98-101
The Flight of Katharina von Bora, (Die Flucht der Katharina von Bora), 30, 44
The Great Female Director, 16, **18-20**
The King and the Quiet in the Land (Der König und die Stille im Lande), 27-8, 70
Hopelessness, 13

Klepper, Jochen: Poetry and Hymnology –
generally, 11, 14-15, 28, 34, 44
Christian poetry and hymnology, **84-92**
hymns and the Bible, 44, 84
hymns and Church's year, 87
hymns, popularity of his, 32
Evangelisches Gesangbuch, 86
'John 15.3' (poem), 91-2
King's Poems, 25-6, 91
Kyrie (anthology), 11, 28, 86
'Morgenlied', 85-6
Nachspiel (poems, essays), 43
Olympic Sonnets, 24-5, 90
Song of Comfort in the Evening, 88-9
Ziel der Zeit (collected poems), 11 n.1

Klepper, Jochen: Prose –
   In Tormentis Pinxit, 27, 50, 58, 80
   Nachspiel (essays, poems), 43
   see also Klepper, Diaries
   see also Klepper, Journalism
   see also Klepper, Novels

Klepper, Jochen: Thought –
   Bible-based living, **93-106,** 107
   Bible, understanding and use of the, 116, 118-119
   Christian leaders, nature of, 22, 51, 63, 71, 82, 110, 117
   Christian writing, nature of **44-83**, 102-103, 118
   Die Losungen, influenced by, **95-106, 117-118**
   house ownership, importance to him of, 29-30
   human, what it means to be, **109-113**
   hymnology, Christian, **84-92**
   Lohmeyer, E., influence of, 14, 108
   Lutheran beliefs, 29, 44-5, 87, 92, 108, 109, 113
   vocation to Christian writing, 29, 83, 117-118
   war and military service, 33-4
   writers, other German Christian, 43

Klepper, Johanna ('Hanni') –
   assisted with Klepper's work, 17, 23, 45, 104
   baptism, 18, 33
   Berlin, living in, 34-5
   birthday, 20, 40
   Breslau, house in, 16, 19, 24
   character, 16, 17
   Christianity, conversion to, 17
   daughters –
      see Stein, Brigitte
      see Stein, Renate
   death, 11, 33, 38, 40-1
   Der Kahn, idea for 45
   Gerstel fashion house, 16
   Jewish, 17, 30, 34, 36
   loans to Klepper, 17
   marriage, 11, 17, 18, 46
   wealth, 17

Langsdorff, H., 37
Leopold, Count, of Ansbach-Dessau, 52-3
Lilge, K., 31
Lohmeyer, E., 14, 108
Lohmeyer, M., 14, 16
Luther, M., 13-14, 27, 29-30, 42, 82, 84, 98, 99, 104, 113, 116
   see also Katharina von Bora
Lutheranism, 44, 59, 68, 74, 87, 92, 108, 109, 113
Mann, O., 43 n.81
Mariendorf Old Church, 18, 97
Mascher, B., 43 n.81
Meschke, K., 30-1, 37, 41, 42, 92
Meschke, E.-J., 30-1, 37, 42 n.77, 92
Moravian Brotherhood, 12 27, 93
   see also *Die Losungen*
Moses, 111
National Socialist Movement, 16, 19, 21, 22, 26, 36, 70, 82, 96
Nikolassee, 28, 31, 32, 33, 36, 41
Oder, River, 12, 20, 35, 45, 46-7, 49, 81

Old Testament, 82, 86, 93, 95, 109-112, 114-115, 116
Old Testament and what it means to be human, **109-115**
Olympic Games (1936), 24-5, 90
Otto, W., 14
Pesne, A., 59
Peter the Great of Russia, 55-7, 60
Pietism, Pietists, 14, 15, 27-8, 70
Poland, 12, 13
Potsdam, 21, 50, 57, 66, 68, 70, 79
Protestantism, 59, 74, 77, 97, 108
Protestant Press Agency, 15, 20, 30
Ragotin *alias* Frederick William I, 69, 70, 71
Reformation, the, 92, 108-110
Reformation Day, 92
Reichsschrifttumskammer - *see* State Literary Chamber
Reske, H., 120
Riemschneider, E. G., 15n.6, 16n.8,
Scarron, P., 69
Schneider, R., 11, 21-2, 28, 29, 43
Schröder, R. A., 43
Seidel, I., 43
Silesia, 13, 15, 19, 33, 49
Silesian Broadcasting Co., 15
Social Democratic Party, 16, 19
Sophie Dorothea of Hanover, 53, 54, 56, 63, 66, 69, 70, 72, 73, 74, 76-7
Soviet Republic, 34-5
Speer, A., 28
Stalingrad, 39, 40
State Literary Chamber, 26, 95, 100, 101, 102, 103
Stehmann, S., 43
Stein, Brigitte - 16, 19, 21, 31, 32, 45, 99
Stein, Johanna – *see* Klepper, Johanna
Stein, Renate ('Reni') - 11, 16, 34-5, 45, 99
 baptism, 33
 birthday, 38
 death, 33, 41-2
 emigration attempts, 31, 32-3, 37-8, 39, 40, 41
 factory work, 36, 38, 40
 yellow star, 36
Stettin (Szczecin), 12, 46, 54
Stralsund, 54
Sweden, 31, 33, 37, 38-41, 54
Swedish community, Berlin, 37
Switzerland, 18, 32, 38
Tappolet, W., 32
Taube, O. von, 43
Thalmann, R., 18
Tobis (film company), 30, 37
Ullstein publishers, 21
Universum Film (UFA), 22-4
Wallmann, J., 82 n.93
Wentorf, R., 121
Wilhemine, Princess, 21, 52, 56, 57, 62, 66-7, 72, 74, 76-8, 80
Wolff, M. (Gottschalk), 37-8
World War I, 13, 99
World War II, 11, 33-5, 99
Würzburg, 39
'Die Zeitwende', 43
Zeuthen, 48-9
Zinzendorf, Nikolaus von, 27-8

Also by J.W. Rogerson

The Poet Prophets of the Old Testament:
Beauchief Abbey Lectures 2017 (2018)

The Case for Ernst Lohmeyer (2017)

Upside-Down Kingdom:
Beauchief Abbey Sermons 2012-2015 (2015)

Cultural Landscapes and the Bible:
Collected Essays (2015)

The Kingdom of God:
Five Lectures (2015)

Perspectives on the Passion (2014)

The Holy Spirit in Biblical and
Pastoral Perspective (2013)

On Being a Broad Church:
An Exploration (2013)

Published by Beauchief Abbey Press
and available from www.lulu.com